Iain MacLeod
FATHERHOOD

✯ ✯ ✯
GET READY FOR LIFE'S GREATEST ADVENTURE

Copyright © 2018 Iain MacLeod

All rights are reserved. You may not distribute this report in any way. You may not sell it, or reprint any part of it without written consent from the author, except for the inclusion of brief quotations in a review.

Cataloguing in Publication details are available from the National Library of Australia www.trove.nla.gov.au

Creator: MacLeod, Iain

Title: Fatherhood: Get Ready for Life's Greatest Adventure / Iain MacLeod

ISBN: 978-0-646-96655-7 (paperback)
ISBN: 978-0-6482441-0-3 (mobi)
ISBN: 978-0-6482441-1-0 (epub)

Cover design & layout: Spiffing Covers
Editing: Shelley Kenigsberg

Printed: IngramSpark (Worldwide)

For more information on Iain MacLeod, see:
www.lovepirates.com.au

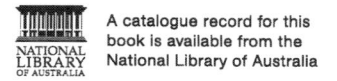

A catalogue record for this book is available from the National Library of Australia

Contents

1. Introduction 5
2. First Of All, I'm From Glasgow 7
3. The Time Bomb 17
4. Ok Let's Go For It 23
5. Hungover In Miami 36
6. So, We're Having A Baby 42
7. The First Scan 50
8. Woo Hoo! Tell The World 59
9. A Wandering Mind 63
10. Last Chance Saloon 73
11. Thirty-Two Weeks, And A Wee Scare 83
12. Calm Birth, Calm Life 88
13. Life Interrupted 93
14. Here We Go 99
15. Life Begins 112
16. Home 117
17. One Month: A Different World 122
18. Two Months: Sleep Deprivation Dreams 126

19. Three Months: Throw In A Hand Grenade 135
20. Four Months: It's All I Can Remember 139
21. Five Months: Now We're Getting Into It 142
22. Six Months: Illness And Glycerin 153
23. Intermission 157
24. Seven Months: Round The World And Back 161
25. Eight Months: Separation Anxiety 177
26. Nine Months: I'm On The Outside 182
27. Ten Months: Through The Wars 187
28. Eleven Months: Back To Reality 208
29. Twelve Months: Down And Almost Out 213
30. And We're Only Getting Started 219
31. Epilogue: 40 Years Down 222
32. Sources 226

1

Introduction

Twenty years ago I took out a student loan to 'further my education'. I bought a tent, a rucksack and a one-way flight to Greece. One month later I was sitting in a Police Station staring down the barrel of a gun.

I thought I'd seen a bit of life, as it turns out, I hadn't seen shit.

This is my story of becoming a father. Starting with the drawn-out process it took to make the decision to go for it, through the pregnancy, the main event and all the way up to the first birthday party.

It's not an instruction manual, although I *will* try and give you a straight answer on how much it's likely to cost. It's what I learned and what—with the benefit of hindsight—I would have done differently.

It's the good, the bad, the freakin' amazing and the downright terrifying. Some of the funniest, the most disheartening and without a doubt, the most joyful moments I've ever experienced. It's real life and all the imperfections that come with it, and if you're thinking about having a kid, it's a wee taster of what might be ahead.

Granted every person, every baby and every journey is different, but no matter where you've been or what you've done with your time—nothing, is anything like this. For some it's an awful lot harder than it was for us; for most I think, a lot easier. Nevertheless it's a trip like no other, and one that I highly recommend.

Consider this, if you were going to travel round Africa for six months you'd buy a guidebook, read up, get some facts. Maybe even learn some language beforehand. This book will help you on that front, a little bit.

But if you wanted to know what it was actually going to be like when you got there. What the Congo River smells like as the sun comes up, how the locals react to you the further you stray from the beaten path, and how the journey itself changes you, as a person? Well, you'd need a different kind of book—it's a bit more like that, I think.

Now I'm hardly a pioneer in this endeavour. Fatherhood is a well-trodden path for sure, but on the other hand it's not something men talk about very much. If they did I wouldn't have made so many mistakes, and you wouldn't be reading this right now.

So, enough, here you go. Here's your preview, pay attention, take heed, and enjoy.

2

First Of All, I'm From Glasgow

"There's no such thing as bad weather, just the wrong clothing, so get yourself a sexy raincoat and live a little."
—Billy Connolly. **Surprisingly good fatherhood advice too, a little preparation goes a long way!**

Allow me to set the scene, wind the clock back so you can understand where I'm coming from, and why—I think—I resisted the idea of having kids for so long.

First of all, I'm from Glasgow.

No, it's not a reason for not wanting kids, but it might explain my tendency to swear, my disregard for authority, and, as you'll discover in the coming pages, my indignation at anyone trying to tell me what to do. Three traits that are not particularly useful for a first time parent I might add.

I was born in Glasgow in 1974, my mum was 23, and my dad was 30 at the time—both a lot younger than I am now. Dad was an aspiring visual artist (graphic designer before the 'label' existed) doing all right for himself in a brand new industry and my mum worked in a photographic studio. On their first date he picked her up in his E-type and they went for a fondue. Flash bugger.

Fast forward a couple of years and my childhood pictures look like something out of 'Anchorman'. Shag-pile rugs, brown corduroy flairs, turtlenecks and curly hair. That's me *and* my dad. But with my dad you could throw in chunky gold bracelets, rings, and the hairy chest. The 70s. Brilliant. I would have my day though.

The first movie my mum took me to was 'The Jungle Book'. At the next, 'Star Wars', Mum says it was the first time she ever saw an audience stand up and clap at the end of a film. Pretty good going for the hard-to-please Glasgow audiences (although Chewbacca does look like he came from Glasgow).

I only have flashes of memories from those early years. I ran away from home on a number of occasions, even ran away from school once. In fact my earliest memory is one of my little feet in my dad's big slippers—running, or shuffling—away from home. It's like an old photograph, imprinted in my mind

I took off at the age of two wearing my all-in-one babygro and my dad's slippers, heading down the street to see if my friend Claire Crichton was around. Barry, her father, was in the driveway when I arrived and announced, "Hello, I'm here to play for a long time my mummy knows."

I guess I was an adventurous little fella right from the start. Only now can I imagine the shock my parents must have received when they answered the phone. "Iain? No he's downstairs in the... Iain!"

But it's the 80s I remember most. The decade of Bruce Springsteen and Michael Jackson, 'Back to the Future' and 'Miami Vice'. When turning your collar up was cool, the piano tie had its five minutes of fame and, for a couple of years, loads of Scottish kids had the misfortune of walking around in tartan jeans. And they say the 70s was the decade that style forgot.

The 80s were my formative years: from six through to 16, and I crammed a lot in: sports of all description, musical pursuits, artistic endeavours, girls and alcohol. A whole lot of fun, and quite a lot of trouble. Most of the time I didn't get caught though. At the time I liked to think I was outsmarting my parents and the teachers. Not so sure about that now.

Nevertheless there was trouble, but not in a rebellious way, just mischief, just for kicks. I had a great childhood, a great family life. I was lucky enough to have visited Asia, America, the Middle East and we'd been all over Scotland of course. We'd even ventured into England a couple of times.

And so, my parents shouldn't have been that surprised when I told them I wasn't going to finish my last year of school, I was going to America instead. I was 16. I'd done well enough at the end of fifth year to get into university, so sixth year was a waste of time as far as I was concerned. A poster in the corridor at school read: 'Academic year in the USA' and off I went.

I asked to go to the West Coast—thinking California, beaches, learning to surf, and chicks… mostly chicks really. I ended up in Medford, Oregon. West indeed but not exactly the Surfers Paradise I was expecting. More Wild West than the OC unfortunately.

Oregon is just north of California. But Medford was nowhere near the coast. Still, it *is* the safest place to be in the USA should there ever be a nuclear war. So that was good. Mother was happy about that. It's something to do with the slight dip 'valley' it's in, the mountains, the prevailing winds, and probably because there's pretty much fuck all there worth concerning yourself with. Unless the Russians were overly pissed off with the diabolical movie 'Look Who's Talking' and decided to send a nuke over specifically for Kirstie Alley who lived locally. A bit severe really, but maybe after 'Look

Who's Talking Too'? That was a *very* bad movie. Somebody should have been shot, at least, for that one.

I had a good time though; I was an exchange student and I loved it. American high school lived up to all the stereotypes too—teenage angst, cheerleaders, jocks, the alternative kids and the geeks. I went to the prom, got a letterman's jacket and a chick. The whole deal.

I came home after Oregon and studied at the University of Glasgow. Two years of psychology, then I moved into management studies and worked as a lifeguard, a swimming teacher and a wine waiter. And a couple of years later the travel bug returned, so I took out a student loan and buggered off to Greece.

It was the first time I'd done the solo travel thing, and I was a little nervous to begin with but soon settled into it. I loved meeting people from all over the world. Most of us reasonably like-minded, just looking for a bit of adventure. It was liberating to realise you could take off anywhere on your own and be absolutely fine.

After a couple of weeks I ended up on the island of Eos, where Alan, a good friend from Glasgow, was working for the summer. Alan's 21st birthday came around so he took the day off work, and we put our drachmas together to fund a day of beach, boozing and whatever else. Unfortunately, 'whatever else' turned out to be a night in a jail cell, the aforementioned gun and an eviction from the island. What was I saying about being absolutely fine?

Over dinner we'd been joking with our waitress; she was cute, and we were all having a laugh. The owner of the restaurant got the wrong end of the stick however, then he belted the two of us in the face with it. We looked at each other, thought 'Oh shit' and ran for the door. Alan made it. I didn't.

They sat me in a corner, emptied the restaurant and then the entire staff started kicking the shit out of me. I curled up on the ground until, eventually, a policeman arrived and I breathed a sigh of relief. Then he got stuck in too. 'Fuck, here we go', I thought, and assumed the fetal position once again. When the kicking stopped I was marched off to the station for a more clinical beating, along with an interrogation as to where, and who, my friend was. It came to an end when one of them unclipped the holster on his hip, and laid a hand on his gun 'We'll deal with you later.' I was told, as they helped me into my 3x2 cell for the evening. At least they'd stopped hitting me. You gotta look on the bright side.

The next morning I was escorted through to the Chief's office, and this time the gun was out the holster, and actually pointed at me. Now despite the fact that it's a more threatening gesture, it didn't have quite the same effect as it had the day before. It was still confronting, and mildly terrifying, but I suspected we were coming to the end of this little episode.

I didn't think they were going to pull the trigger. I was convinced they were bluffing. 'If they shoot me here it will make an awful mess,' I thought. 'Surely, if they were going to do that, they would have done it in the cell, where a hose would have easily cleaned it all up.'

I was told to leave the island; if I ever appeared on Eos again, they would kill me.

As oddly confident as I was that they weren't about to shoot me there and then, I had no desire to give them a chance to change their mind. I was offski. I walked out the front door of the Police Station on my own, straight down to the port and on to a fast ferry to Piraeus.

It felt, freakin', amazing. As that ferry pulled away and I watched the little port diminish in size I had the most amazing rush of adrenalin. I was alive. I'd made it, and at that moment in time, I felt as if I could have done, fucking, anything. And far from discouraging me from further travel, I'm sure it only encouraged me. My poor mother. No child of mine is ever going to Greece, especially on their own.

Eventually I made it back to Glasgow, finished my final year of university and worked in a printing factory for a couple of months. It all seemed rather mundane. I kept my eyes open for another opportunity to travel and when I heard that Boulder Rugby Club were looking for players—I jumped at the chance. On 5 September 1995, I headed off to Boulder Colorado to play rugby.

It's easy to look back and say that certain events changed your life, but that was an important trip for me. If Greece had given me a taste for adventurous travel, then Boulder gave me the inkling that I might not even go back to Glasgow afterwards. Maybe it really was a one-way ticket this time.

Boulder was great fun. I ended up living and working with a bunch of other 'funny talkers' as the Americans called us: some Kiwis, a few English guys, and me—a Scot. All of us playing rugby, working in construction and living pretty much day-to-day. We had a ball, and I'm still in touch a couple of the guys from back then.

I played a full season in Boulder, then it seemed as if this little period of life was coming to its natural end. A lot of the guys were moving on and I decided to do the same. My dad and my sister were planning a holiday in the Dominican Republic, and I saved up and flew over to join them. After they returned to Scotland I stayed on in Puerto Plata and rented an apartment.

I made some friends, started learning Spanish and looked into work. Before I could get too comfortable however, my

Grandfather died. It was completely out of the blue, for me at least anyway, and I was rocked. I just had to go home.

I'd gone round to see my Grandpa before I left for Colorado. For the first time ever he suggested we go out for a dram in a wee local pub. It was dark, dingy, with only a few old fella's sitting up at the bar. Silence when they noticed us, and then.

"Ah Billy, how you doing? The usual?"

"Yep. This is my grandson, Iain."

"Ahh, hi. I'll have the same please."

We had a couple of whiskies then headed back. It was great. I'd never done anything like that with him before.

My Grandpa had been in the Second World War and spent most of his time over in India. He was in the Royal Scot's Grey's and looked after tanks and horses—the cavalry. After the war he worked at IBM and after retirement had taken his mechanical knowledge to help out in a local garage in the afternoons. The garage was next door to the pub we were sitting in, and now I was discovering why he enjoyed working there so much.

If it wasn't for the Second World War I wouldn't even be here. My Grandpa was from Aberdeen and whilst in India he became good friends with a Glaswegian, Alec. The two war heroes came back on leave just once. My Grandpa met Alec's sister Mary, and she was waiting for him two years later when the war was finally over. You don't hear stories like that anymore.

And I certainly heard plenty of stories from my Grandpa; we visited my grandparents most weekends when I was a kid. My abiding memory from that time was of sitting with him as he told me about the war, about horses and tanks and giant spiders, taught me how to box, and how to catch a scorpion. Exotic stories and the skills to match. What a legend.

The last thing he said to me that day when I dropped him off was "Make sure you go and see everything you can son, go and do, everything."

I didn't know it would be the last time I would ever see him. But in some way I'm kind of glad it was. I can remember that, not him sick in a hospital bed. So I came home from the Dominican Republic when my Grandpa died, but it wasn't long before I was off again.

I worked in the newspaper industry for a couple of years and although it was an interesting experience, it wasn't quite the experience I was looking for. I wanted to do something to help, and if I could do it somewhere exotic, all the better.

So I kept my eyes open, and what I found was nothing less than the fulfillment of a childhood dream. Having watched so many David Attenborough documentaries growing up, I couldn't believe it when I discovered a coral reef protection program that took me to Africa. The southern coast of Tanzania to be specific.

The project I worked on resulted in the establishment of the Mnazi Bay–Ruvuma Estuary Marine Park, and all these years later I'm still rather proud of that. I learned to speak Swahili in Tanzania, and afterwards took off round Africa. From there it was on to the British Virgin Islands (the BVI), and once again it was family reasons that eventually brought me back to Glasgow.

This time I hung around a lot longer than expected, because I met a beautiful Irish student, Erin. We met at a strip joint one night. Well, not really, it was an old pub in Glasgow where there happened to be a stripper. Erin liked my laugh, I liked her smile. She had a lovely Irish lilt; I sounded like… a Glaswegian. She was gorgeous and I was punching above my weight. We're quite different in many ways but you know the story. We hit it off.

My great sense of humour helped. Of course.

Erin is from Ballyfin—a tiny wee place in the countryside an hour from Dublin. She's the second youngest of six siblings (two brothers and four sisters). She's a country girl who loves the city; I'm a city boy who loves the country. Her stories of growing up revolved around the farm, kids running around having a riot, playing shop in the peat barn, countless cousins all over the place and the odd crazy neighbour thrown in. She grew up in a fairly small world I suppose, geographically speaking, until she went to University College Dublin to study radiography.

After graduating she stayed in Dublin and worked as a radiographer. Then she and her sister Niamh, and a friend, Patricia, bought round-the-world tickets and set off on a trip. They had a great time traveling and working their way around the globe, through the states, the Pacific Islands, Australia and then Asia.

When Erin returned to Ireland she found it hard to settle. She couldn't quite face going back to radiography so found a post-grad course in IT, which lead her to Glasgow, and me. A year into the course she was invited to a birthday party at an old pub called The Doublet. It was going to be a laugh she was told; the birthday boy had no idea there was going to be a stripper. Sure, she thought, why not.

And that was that.

A few years later when we decided to get out of Glasgow, and Erin suggested we go to Sydney, my thoughts were exactly the same. Sure, why not. Let's go.

I know it's quite a roundabout way of getting there, but I hope all of this helps explain the terror that consumed me when faced with the prospect of having a kid.

I guess you could say I like to travel. I like the excitement and the freedom of picking up and leaving, with nothing but a few bucks in the bank account, a rucksack on my back and the brains in my head to get me into, and keep me out of trouble at the same time. I don't think that's a particularly unusual frame of mind.

But a kid? What? That's game over. No more adventures now Iain. That's it. Oh sure it'd be nice to have kids… eventually, sure. But not now… Shit.

3

The Time Bomb

"The true genius of a Woman is her subtle flair in creating the illusion that you are the smart one."
—Josh Stern. **Difficult to admit, but…**

The subject of children arose for the first time a couple of years ago. Erin brought it up.

I'd say this is the way it happens in most cases. You're happily getting on with your life, you've met, courted and moved in together. It's worked out and you might be married. If not, chances are the law sees it that way. You've settled into a nice life, both working away at your careers, enjoying nights out and weekends with friends. Holidays, trips and traveling thrown in as often as possible, spending time relaxing and enjoying each other's company. Lovely.

Then somebody mentions children, and from that moment on it's a ticking time bomb. Doesn't matter how long you've been together, if one person wants children and the other doesn't, you're screwed. It's either going to happen or the party's over.

Just to add to the sweeping generalisations, it seems as if women are in more of a hurry to procreate than men. The 'Let's have a child' conversations are seldom initiated by blokes. Not that I've had a lot of them. There's not exactly a long line of women knocking down my door wanting kids. But from asking around it's almost always the women who start the ball rolling.

Now I know, however, that after the age of 35 it becomes considerably more difficult for women to get pregnant, and if they do there's a much greater chance of carrying children with Down syndrome, or a range of other genetic disorders. I'm sure this plays into their thinking.

Men are also less willing to give up their lives, I think, especially when everything's in order and going so well. It's probably an evolutionary thing. Good excuse anyway, prevents me from facing up to the fact that I can be a selfish bastard sometimes.

It's not like Erin was one of those women who just *couldn't wait* to have kids, but for most women I'd say there comes a time, when it's just time.

Erin introduced children into the conversation very carefully. It was only briefly mentioned, as something that she would like, at some point in the not too distant future. Not the immediate future, but in a while.

We'd moved to Australia together and it had worked. We both knew that marriage was on the cards, although I'd not plucked up enough courage to pop the question yet. Children too, I suppose, were inevitable. We'd been together for about seven years by this point. Fair enough.

I imagine our conversation was reasonably typical. I didn't say a lot, Erin talked while I probably looked at my feet a bit. She didn't mention it again for a long time.

After that initial talk, or more accurately, talking to, the whole idea was shut out of my mind for a good few months. Complete head-in-the-sand approach. Very effective for a short period of time, and I could continue pretending that my life wasn't about to change completely.

Six months down the line however, it's mentioned again. I'm actually quite surprised it's taken this long to come up. She's a clever one my wife (yes, she's now my wife) and yet again it's a short conversation. Erin knows how to play me. I can be a stubborn bugger when I want to be and backing me into a corner wouldn't do anyone any good. So, cunning like a freakin' fox she bides her time. Periods of grace are given, dates are set to return to the conversation.

God, I sound like hard work.

Anyway, throughout all of this I allow the idea into my mind more often, and I play around with it. Sometimes it's not so bad. Then the fact that it's not so bad scares the crap out of me and I close it down again.

Each time it's allowed into my mind it causes less alarm though. Got to be a good sign. I suppose it's a bit like those contractions I've heard about. They happen very occasionally to begin with, then more and more frequently, eventually you're in labour and then there's a baby.

This is the sort of shit that frequently ran through my mind.

"Everybody who has a kid seems to be permanently exhausted. People just disappear. I can forget about having a life. It'll cost a fortune. Why on earth does anyone bother? It's a wonder any of us are here at all. Why is it that people only talk in negatives whenever babies are mentioned? I'm sure there must be good bits. I suppose I know deep down it will be a great thing.

It'll change my life and all that. I like my life the way it is though. It changes your priorities… Well that's a bit scary, what's wrong with my priorities the way they are? And why is it that some people just go ahead and fire them out non—stop, and sometimes at such an early age? Have they not thought it through? Am I just being incredibly selfish? Well, there are things I want to do in life that I can forget about when I have a baby.

Determination and patience

But, wait a minute, if you really want to do something, all you have to do is set your mind to it, combine determination with patience and you can do almost anything you like. Having a baby shouldn't get in the way… or, is that just a load of bullshit? I can see the beleaguered father sitting there laughing at me and my ignorance—"Aha ha, what does he know. That's what I used to think."

"You just don't know how it's going to pan out until you do it, that's the thing. I like sleep. I like peace and quiet. I don't like loud noises. I like having time to myself."

Pretty self-indulgent stuff, but not unusual for a bloke contemplating parenthood I would imagine.

I laid it all out.

Against. I'm shit scared. I like things the way they are. There are things I want to do with my life. We can't afford it. We're not ready. I'm shit scared. It's grown up stuff and I don't want to grow up.

For. I like the idea of having kids. I don't want to be too old when I have children. I'd like to be able to enjoy them, play football with them. Also, it'd be nice to have someone to look after us when we're old. Lots of parents have loads of fun with their kids when they're grown up. You hear people say their kids are their best friends.

A while ago I read an interview with Jeff Bridges, the actor. He said exactly that; how he was a bit of an asshole when he first got married, he was almost dragged into having kids and now realises it's the best thing he's ever done. I enjoy my own parents' company, they're like friends and I'm sure they feel the same way about my sister and me.

When you look at it like that, the 'against' doesn't really stack up very well. After months of rolling it around in my head I eventually had to give myself a serious talking to.

"There's stuff you want to do in life. Really? Well are you doing it right now? Why not? Either go and fucking do it, or get over yourself and stop using that as an excuse. You're scared? Man up. Not ready? Nobody ever is. Man up.

Want some more? OK. You're getting older and you can't be bothered going out like you used to. You don't mind a night in on a Friday night. You're up at 7am on the weekends looking forward to a kayak, a hike or a swim—couldn't even lie in if you wanted to. You like to make the most of the day. Listen to yourself, like to make the most of the day? What the fuck?! And you're not even embarrassed by that kind of statement? You're a freakin' father already!"

I'm sure it's different for everyone, but I guess I had to resolve it before flicking that mental switch. Sometimes I can make incredibly quick decisions—and I'm happy dealing with the consequences if it's not the right move. But other times, it takes me months of mulling things over to resolve the turmoil in my mind.

I thought, back then, there was no point in becoming a father if my heart wasn't in it. Now I can safely say that once that wee person arrives, there's no such thing as halves. You're in. I certainly was.

Ah the mind tricks, the pros and cons… the inevitability. At the most basic level it's what we're here for. It's the whole point of being alive. Survival of the fittest, survival of you, to enable the survival of the species. It drives us more than anything else.

So why was it so difficult to make the decision? With blokes in general, I reckon it comes down to a fear of change; a fear of 'loss of freedom', and a fear of commitment—which is actually the fear of *permanent* change.

This inbuilt drive *not* to commit, probably comes from an innate need of males to spread their seed as widely as possible. Ironic, that the genetic desire to procreate, prevents you from actually wanting to procreate.

Yet, of course, without this genetic encouragement none of us would be here at all. Nature wins out despite the most ardent and determined of blokes trying to convince themselves that everything's fine the way it is, and there is no need to have kids. Nature finds its way and we're off into the unknown.

It's kind of like the first day at school. You have no idea what to expect. You've never been near anything even close to school before, so you've no frame of reference.

At my age now, however, when you've been around a bit, there's not really that much that you don't know a *little* something about. Maybe that's not the best way of putting it—there's not much you don't know how to handle, how to deal with.

Fatherhood, becoming a parent, having a baby however, how on earth do you deal with that? No frame of reference. Nothing to compare it with.

In fact, here's a comparison that might work. It's a bit like bungee jumping—terrifying and exciting all at the same time. You're not so sure you're ready for it, but somehow, you're standing on the edge of a bridge. Someone you've never met before says jump—and off you go.

It's once you've taken the jump however… that's when it starts to get interesting.

4

OK Let's Go For It

"Go to the edge of the cliff and jump off. Build your wings on the way down."
—Ray Bradbury. **Easier said than done, but in the end it's the only choice.**

The decision is made. Let's try and have a baby.

It can take quite a while for some people to conceive—months, even years. Erin seems to think it will be difficult for her. So in case we can't actually manage it ourselves, we discuss our options.

I don't know a huge amount about IVF, but I know there are needles and injections involved. We both know people who've been through it. It sounds awful. Emotionally taxing for both parties and not too freaking cheap either. Not too sure we'd like to go down that route, so we decide if we don't have any luck, adoption is the way to go. So, now that's out of the way we can get on with something I do know about—making babies.

Or so I thought.

Believe it or not there are only a couple of days a month that a woman can actually get pregnant. A window. And much to my surprise, even on those days nothing is guaranteed. So what you have to do is hang back, wait, bide your time and pretend everything is normal, then go for it like rabbits when the window arrives.

Now on the periphery of my consciousness, I can almost remember Erin having mentioned something about windows before; I remember a woman from the natural contraception society in the 'So you're going to get married' course telling us about various methods of contraception too.

Apart from just not having sex, natural contraception, I remember, also had something to do with windows and cycles. There were charts and tables, and something about mucus. The rest is completely blanked from my memory. Thank God.

In typical male fashion, however, I don't really believe any of that bollocks (or didn't back then). If you have sex without condoms you get pregnant. It's as simple as that. Yet again, I was happy to go with the head in the sand approach until I absolutely had to pull my head, ahem, out. I think a wee bit more knowledge up front however, would have helped me understand at least the odds, and statistics behind it all. But, as I've mentioned, taking advice isn't really my strong suit.

Anyway the business of having a baby, once you get into it—is exactly that—a business. It's not very romantic. In fact, as I know now, there's not that much about the whole baby business that is.

Conversations like this were all too common:

"Come on Iain, before it gets late and we're too tired."

"I'm already tired, I can't be bothered, can we not just give it a miss tonight? We'll do it tomorrow morning before work."

"No, we won't, come on."

It doesn't matter whether you've both worked late and are exhausted, whether you're in the huff with each other, whatever… you're at it.

As a teenager, I'd never, ever have imagined having conversations like that. Yet here we are. Jees, what sort of conversations am I going to be having in another 10 years? Shit. Doesn't bear thinking about.

Anyway, unless conception happens straight away, as it does for some people, you find yourself going through this month after month after month. And anyone who finds themselves in this position will eventually stumble across the irony that they've spent their entire adult life trying to avoid getting someone pregnant, only to discover that when you actually want to do it, it ain't happenin'.

Maybe it was blind ignorance, maybe it was wishful thinking but I was never in any doubt Erin would get pregnant. And before too long, we get what we're hoping for. Well, almost.

It happens right at the beginning of the process. We've only had a couple of rounds of 'going for it' and, we think we've been successful. Unfortunately, success before you're quite ready for it—can be terrifying.

It was a lovely weekend. One that seemed to go on for ages. I caught up with some old workmates on Friday, got nicely drunk, didn't stay out too late. Took it easy on Saturday, had a beer with a couple of folks, went for a kayak, then dinner and a DVD with Erin.

Surfing lesson at Bondi on Sunday morning, round the markets with Erin and her sister, Niamh (in Sydney now, too), a few beers at Icebergs and we even save a life! (Spotted someone in distress and alerted the lifeguards.) We make it home by 6pm and settle in for dinner and telly. Very relaxed, feeling very fulfilled with life in general. Even the specter of work on Monday morning isn't a problem. I've made the most of these two days and it'll be another weekend soon.

Then Erin says, "I don't want to freak you out, but I think I might be pregnant". Oh. Shit. Shouldn't have told me *that* then should you. Fuck, better enjoy these weekends while I can.

"But I don't understand." she follows "There's a window of when it can happen, and that's when you were away... but I'm late."

"Well is that an unusual situation? What?! What do you mean when I was away? How often are you late... have you ever been late before? How often does something like that happen anyway?"

I keep my voice steady, and I'm surprised at how steady I really do feel.

"... Don't know," she says.

Now for a bloke, that answer is almost inconceivable. How could you *not* know? If I'd been through the discomfort of having my period every month since puberty, I think I'd have figured it out by now.

Anyway, it appears that you don't really pay much attention to these things, until you happen to be involved in the process of baby making. Fair enough. I have no basis for comparison, and no idea what I'm talking about.

This, as it turns out, is pretty much commonplace for the foreseeable future.

"So... are there not tests for these things? Shall we go out and get a test from the chemists?"

"I'll do one tomorrow at the hospital. They've got them at work."

"Ah... ok. Are you sure? We're not going to get much sleep tonight."

Just then the phone goes and it's Erin's mum. She disappears into another room to talk, and I'm left there watching 'Dancing with the Stars'. Fuck knows how that ended up on, I was randomly flicking through the channels when Erin started our conversation, and I must have just stopped at some point. So, there it is. Taunting me from the corner—and given this little moment to myself, contemplating the implications of our discussion and feeling a little dazed, I can't quite bring myself to change the channel.

'Dancing with the Stars'. I've never seen more than 10 seconds of it before, but I can't move. Can't even lift a finger.

Now, I'm not sure, but I think my reluctance to use the remote control sitting in the palm of my hand, is because to do so would be openly admitting to myself that on the brink of discovering I am about to become a father—possibly one of the more monumental moments in life—all I'm interested in, is what's on the telly.

So I leave it there. Dancing with the freakin' Stars.

Thankfully Erin comes out the room and I snap back into reality; as unusual a reality as it is. She remembers having bought some 'help-you-get-pregnant' vitamins, and there's a pregnancy test in the pack.

"Well… let's do it then, let's find out. We'll either get a great night's sleep, or we won't sleep a wink! Have you been taking those vitamins by the way?"

"Yeah on and off, for a while I suppose."

"Oh, and you're surprised that you might be pregnant?"

As I've already mentioned, with my simplistic view of how babies are made, I'm not really that surprised that Erin might be pregnant. A little stunned perhaps, but not too surprised.

"Let me know when three minutes are up will you? Start…now" she says.

I write the start time down, not trusting myself to remember 7:40pm.

A long three minutes. I do like it when a weekend goes on forever. We should do this more often…

Not pregnant. Breathe. Breathe. Breathe.

Interesting Sunday night. I'm so emotionally exhausted I take the next day off work. I'm not sure how long I was watching Dancing with the Stars for, but jees, it sure takes it out of you.

I guess these experiences help bring you closer to the reality of it all. Well, maybe not the actual reality, but certainly the real emotions involved; fear, excitement, nervousness, heart-pounding time distorting anticipation, a heady mixture indeed. Actually scarier than standing on the edge of a bridge, and I mean a real fucking bridge, that you're prepared to jump off.

Pregnancy testing: The facts
The first thing you should know is that the pregnancy test kits you buy in chemists are not 100 percent accurate. Can you believe that? Ridiculous, isn't it?

Studies show they *can* be up to about 97 percent accurate, but that's when used by experienced lab technicians. When used by regular folks it falls to 75 percent. This is because we, the human race, are generally stupid and don't know how to follow directions. Over-the-counter pregnancy tests usually consist of a 'strip' that reacts to a couple of drops of urine within a couple of minutes. Most of the kits are looking for HCG (Human chorionic gonadotropin)—a hormone created by the developing embryo about six days after conception, which can be detected in a pregnant woman's urine.

A false negative result can appear if the test has been used before HCG has reached sufficient levels. False positives can happen if the test is past its expiration date, if the user has taken certain drugs, or if they've just failed to follow the instructions.

Even with less than 100% accuracy, it's still relatively simple to find out if you're partner is pregnant. It hasn't always been this easy though. Before the first home test was invented in 1968, the Bufo test was all the rage. Named after the genus of toad that was used. Yes, toad. A female toad was injected with either the serum, or urine from the 'test subject' and if the toad produced eggs within 24 hours, bingo—pregnant.

Before that you had to inject rabbits and baby mice, who were then killed and dissected to see if ovulation had taken place. Nice.

Anyway, if you've done the home test and you're convinced you have a positive result, it's off to the doctor to find out for sure.

So, throughout all of this, the mental gymnastics I'm performing in order to talk myself into it, the decision to go for it and the 'we're trying' phase, I begin to experience a subtle shift in outlook and opinion on all sorts of other things in life. I am preparing myself, I think, to become a parent.

I'll explain, my mobile phone experience kind of sums it up.

For probably 10 years or so I had a basic model mobile phone. When they came on the scene I thought they were brilliant, so handy for work, for life, for pubs, whatever. I jumped in, and as soon as they were affordable I was right in there. Imagine, now, trying to do business without one?

Conversation before mobile phones: "Alright, we'll be in the whisky bar until about 10, then we'll go over to the Wee Chip Pub, after that we might go to The Tunnel, but I can't guarantee it. Look, if we don't go to the Wee Chip, I'll phone Simon, he's not going out tonight, and I'll leave a message with him about where we're off to. No, yeah, I'll try to remember, well, we'll see how it goes…." It was a lottery! Life was a lot more random in those days.

Then mobile phones arrived, and they became pub walky-talkies. I was self-employed at the time so I became a mobile office all of a sudden too. It actually made my type of business possible. My office was the local coffee shop, my car, my bed, and even my actual office occasionally. Superb!

After a few different phones I ended up with the Nokia 3310i. It was an 'almost' waterproof and bump proof phone. I loved it. It never broke like many other phones around me seemed to do. You could drop it in a puddle; even submerge it in a pint, although I was never quite that brave I'm sure it would have been able to handle it. Brilliant. It woke me up in the morning and I could make phone calls—what more could you want or need from a phone?

As other phones became more advanced and acquired further 'unnecessary' functions as far as I was concerned, I stood by my sturdy, and unbreakable Nokia. Camera phones? Who cares? I've got a camera. Why do I need one on my phone?

Even when 3G came along, it proved so disappointing it wasn't worth bothering with. I mean the prospect of being able to talk to other people on a little hand held video system, seemed incredibly tempting. It was 'Star Trek' stuff – the thing of the future – to be able to talk to someone on your own little device, and to be able to see them live on screen? Pretty cool. But no. Actually, still not possible. The 3G system worked like crap, nobody had the bandwidth to be able to carry it off. It was a waste of time and I was going to stick with the Nokia. Until, eventually, my trusted Nokia packed it in completely.

After much deliberation, I jumped full on into the 21st Century and got an iPhone.

Unbelievable. I can't do without it now. I changed my perspective, opened my mind up to something new, and was totally blown away.

I stopped smoking, got back into sports, started working harder than I ever had before and finally got around to learning how to surf. What a difference, and why on earth did it take me so long?

Well, I guess we all get set in our ways now and again. Life can get comfortable, or we just get stuck. We've all been there at some point. In a job, a relationship or a situation we know needs to change. Yet somehow we hang in for longer than we really should, fear of the unknown being stronger than fear of the known perhaps.

With the iPhone I had no choice, but making the decision to have kids, I must admit I was cajoled into it a little bit, and I probably should have done with less cajoling.

Once the decision had been made, however, everything fell into place. Life is more exciting now. More optimistic. Of course, it's also more frightening too, but maybe that's the price of vitality. Not so bad.

In fact, that reminds me. Let me tell you about my granny. She would be 110 if she was alive today, and about 30 years ago my mum bought her a microwave—modern, futuristic devices that were revolutionising kitchens all over the world. We tracked down the easiest to use, simplest microwave we could possibly find. It had a timer and start button. That was all. But could we get her to use it? No, of course not.

She was *so* used to the way things were, that she couldn't open up to the possibility of change. If she had tried, just a little bit things might have been a lot easier for her. But, she was 80 years old and quite entitled to say no to her daughter, or anyone else for that matter. I may well be the same when I'm 80.

But I'm not, yet. Note to self, say yes more often, no – not so much. If only there was a formula for living with less fear.

Oh, and when my Grandpa died we discovered he'd been hiding his whisky in the microwave all these years. Ha! You never know what you might find, if you just open the door and have a look. There was the lesson right there.

Getting pregnant: The facts
As I've said, it's not quite as easy to get pregnant as we've been lead to believe all these years.
    —25% of couples conceive within the first month
    —60% conceive within six months
    —80% conceive within a year.
So 20% of all couples are still struggling after a year. That would become pretty frustrating I can assure you. You would be advised to talk to a professional if you've been at it a year and nothing's happened, that's if you're under 30 and in good shape. If not, then it could be worth seeking advice earlier.

Why it's difficult to get pregnant
1. Timing: There are only a couple of days a month it can happen.
    A woman's pituitary gland goes into overdrive once a month and produces hormones. These hormones trigger the ovaries to release an egg (ovulation) and that solitary egg begins to make its way down one of the fallopian tubes. It's at this exact point in time – you want it to meet some little swimmers coming up in the opposite direction.
    The trick is determining exactly when ovulation is taking place. Now this is really going to be your partner's job, but just so you know—ovulation generally takes place in the midpoint of a woman's cycle, so if she has a consistent 28-day cycle then 14 days after her period begins. That's your time.

It can, however, be variable. Stress and (lots of) exercise can have an effect, so to remove all doubt you can buy an ovulation predictor kit. It tests your partner's urine for the hormones that initiate the whole process, and when you get the green light, off you go.

2. Intelligence: Your sperm are stupid

When a healthy man ejaculates there are upwards of 100 million sperm sent off on their journey. Not a bad start you might think, however, more than 60% of them are sub-standard, and not up to the task. Of the remaining 40 million or so, only about 50 make it through to where the egg *may* be waiting for them. Just 50! The other 39,999,950 sperm swim off in the wrong direction and get lost. The odds are pretty shocking.

Even upon arrival, it's not guaranteed they'll be able to finish the job.

The woman's egg is only available for fertilisation between 12 and 24 hours per cycle, so the sperm might arrive ready to rock n' roll and the egg is closed for business.

One little trick they do have up their sleeves, is that they can lie in wait for about five days. So, if they arrive early, they can hang around waiting for the egg to turn up.

If you're both fit, active and live healthy lifestyles it improves your chances of conceiving. The usual suspects of alcohol, tobacco and caffeine are all detrimental to the process. But there are vitamin supplements that can help you both out.

Take note however, although men produce millions of sperm every day, it takes three months to produce them from scratch, so your increased vitamin intake won't actually benefit your little fellas until three months down the line.

3. Risks: It's a long road

Even when one of your high achievers fertilises an egg there are no guarantees.

When the egg is penetrated it becomes an embryo—a single cell that has to divide and duplicate millions of times before implanting into the uterine wall. It's only once this happens—generally about six days after the initial fertilisation—that conception is considered to have occurred.

Even after that, there's only a 50% percent chance the little subdivided embryo hanging tightly onto the uterine wall will actually make the grade. Apparently, up to half will pass out with the next period in what is referred to as an 'unnoticed miscarriage'.

Of the 50% percent that do hang in there, 20% of those will end up miscarrying within the first three months. You would *not*, want to bet on these odds.

Here's the summary:

—1 egg a month, at a variable time

—Only 50 out of 100,000,000 sperm complete the journey

—12–24 hours' window for the egg to be receptive

—50% chance of immediate miscarriage; 20% chance thereafter.

It really is a miracle any of us are here at all.

Position, position, position

Believe it or not, there are sexual positions that have actually been scientifically tested to see how effective they are in producing babies. The definition of effectiveness was not actual babies however, it was how far into the cervix the sperm were launched—measured using magnetic resonance imaging (MRI).

The results showed the missionary position, and doggy style do the trick. They were also, however, the only two positions tested. I don't know quite what to make of that, except I've been in a MRI scanner before, and they're pretty small... I'll leave it there.

5

Hungover In Miami

"Travel is not really about leaving our homes, but leaving our habits."
—Pico Iyer. **Might be a bit of truth in that.**

Christmas, 2009. Australia virtually shuts down over the period and I'm forced to take at least two weeks off work, so we decide to take three weeks' instead.

Things are always busy before a break: getting everything in place, making sure nothing goes wrong while I'm away. However this time I land a tender for a massive new client so it's even more frantic than usual. It's not long after the global financial crisis and things are tight. Winning this work could help me hang onto my job, so it becomes my obsession, and for the month of December I can safely say I completely forget about babies. Can't say that for much of January though.

We have a great trip planned—Vegas, Fort Lauderdale, New Year at South Beach in Miami and a couple of days in Costa Rica. Relaxation, fun, adventure and lots of catching up with family and old friends. Exactly what life is about.

Half way through this grand trip, sitting on a park bench in South Beach Miami I find out I am going to be a father. It's the 1st January 2010, and I'm feeling pretty sorry for myself after Hogmanay, filled with the sort of self-loathing that follows a serious bevvy. Then a couple passes with a little kid in a pram.

"I'm even looking forward to having a kid, I know I don't say it or talk about it that often, but I really am."

"Well that's just as well, because I'm pregnant."

"Oh my God, really?! Oh my God. How long have you known?"

"Just since yesterday, I didn't tell you … I didn't want to ruin last night."

"Oh my God." and so on…

What a way to start the decade.

I must admit I shed a few tears. Hung over, I'm prone to the odd tear even watching Sunday movies, so this comes as no surprise to Erin either.

"Oh my God."

I'm still feeling shit, and dreadfully hung over although now I'm glowing inside, elated. It is an unusual mixture of emotional high, and severe physical discomfort. Not one I would recommend, but there you go—going to be a daddy. I think I was actually better prepared when we had that false alarm. Life is full of surprises. Erin, of course, is over the moon. Happy that we can actually get pregnant and relieved, but also nervous, about what's ahead.

We get back to Fort Lauderdale later that day (where we're staying with my mum) and we hold onto our secret. We're not sure when, or who we should tell to begin with (if anyone at all) until the three-month scan. Although I know nothing about babies right now, I've been around enough pregnant women to know that you should probably wait for three months before telling anyone. The very next day however, the decision is taken out of our hands.

This is the Costa Rica part of the trip. Where we visit

our friends, Fraser and Jane, who own a rafting business in a tiny wee place called Turrialba.

Russell picks us up at the airport and tells us about the two days of rafting and kayaking he has planned, then he throws in, "Oh, you're not pregnant by the way, are you? Because if you are you shouldn't do any of this."

I just look at Erin and we both smile. "Actually, yeah, I am," she says.

And there it is, it's out there.

Fraser is an old friend from Glasgow and like me, he'd never been that keen on hanging around in Scotland. So he joined me in Africa all those years ago, and we made our way over to the British Virgin Islands. We worked on boats and in bars, and eventually, Fraser met Jane—an extremely capable Kiwi who could look after herself better than Fraser and I put together.

They married, ran a business in the BVI for a while then moved to New Zealand and opened a B&B. And six years ago, they bought a rafting business in Turrialba—Costa Rica Rios.

It was great to catch up with him after so long. We're very similar Fraser and I, and we were both kind of heading in the same direction for a while. I guess some would describe it as an alternative lifestyle, certainly not the nine to five.

For example, we both used to work on an island where there's actual pirate treasure buried—indeed, the very island that inspired Robert Louis Stephenson's *Treasure Island*. It has no electricity and not a computer in sight, but somewhere, there's treasure. Fraser still lives that kind of life. When I called him once I got a message saying he'd taken off into the jungle for a couple of days. And it's real jungle we're talking about here, untouched, virgin rainforest. Although I'm very happy about where I am right now, I do find myself a little jealous when I hear that kind of shit.

Anyway, despite that fact that it's only a short trip, we have a very relaxing time in Costa Rica. Fraser and Jane have a one-year-old, Archie, and they're happy to discuss it all and help us get excited about what is ahead.

For me, it's also good to see my friends with a kid in what is most certainly not, first-world conditions. It shows me that it *can* be done. If I want to, and more importantly, can persuade my lovely wife into it, we can jump back into that kind of lifestyle again further down the line.

They're also quite happy to throw us in at the deep end in regards to parenting. As soon as we arrive at their home, Fraser and Jane have guests to deal with, so they hand us wee Archie (and their mutt) and tell us to get on with it.

So not much more than 24 hours after finding out we're going to be parents—we're saddled with a screaming kid, dog, pram, the works.

And I must say, as a first attempt at parenting… it is a disaster. We do alright for ten seconds or so. Manage to make it as far as the patio door—however trying to open the latch is where it all starts to go wrong. Ten seconds.

The latch is, well let's just politely say it's a real pain in the ass and by the time I've figured it out, the wee man starts to cry. Fair enough, he's probably just frustrated with this idiot his father has landed him with, a fool who can't even open a door. Once I finally manage it we begin herding all the gear, Archie, and the mutt through the gate, and in the middle of the kerfuffle a bag rolls off into the bushes. Then the wee fella *really* starts to cry. Jesus.

I pick him up, Erin heads after the dog who has run away by now, and as I shake little Archie to get him to quiet down, I turn around to see how Erin's getting on. Now my back's turned the pram, of course, rolls off the fucking path, spilling the shopping (including tonight's dinner and the contents of Erin's wallet) all over the ground. Jesus Christ! How difficult can things get in under a minute?

When we do, eventually, corral the mutt into the house along with all the shopping, the pram, and the wee man's welly boots that have fallen off, we sit down and look at each other in shock. Phew. Sigh. Fucking hell.

It's not over yet though. Wee Archie is still yelling at the top of his lungs. So I continue to shoogle him, completely unaware of what to do to stop the racket and then he remembers he's dealing with the guy who can't even open a freakin' door. So he decides to give me a hand.

Archie points at his room. Excellent, let's go to your room then wee man. Now he's pointing at his cot. Great, this'll be easy.

"Hey Erin this guy knows exactly what he wants, he wants to go to bed!"

Into the cot he goes, now he's pointing at his feet, off with the socks, more pointing, up with the blanket. Next he directs me to pull up the guardrail so he can't fall out, then the mosquito net comes down, finally off goes the light and I back myself into the living room.

"Jesus, Erin, that was unbelievable, I've never been ordered around like that before in my life. What a clever little fucker!"

As all of this is going on the crying slows, and finally stops. So I've obviously done the right thing. Fraser walks in about five minutes later and asks where Archie is.

"I put him to bed, it was unreal, he virtually ordered me around, even got me to take of his freaking socks!"

"In his bed! Jesus, it's far too early for his bed, he'll be up all night if you put him to bed now!"

Oh. Lesson number one. Babies are sneaky little fuckers.

After too short a time with old friends talking about life, babies, good times and growing up, we're back on a flight to Fort Lauderdale—and we decide to tell my mum. We are only going to be in the US for a couple more days and it will be more exciting to tell her now, rather than over the phone later on.

It is Erin's birthday at the beginning of January too. I'd bought her a book called *The big book of 60,000 baby names,* and when I hand it to my mum for a look she can't believe it. She had no idea there could be that many names.

6

So, We're Having A Baby

"Most of us become parents long before we have stopped becoming children."
—Mignon McLaughlin. **Yes indeed.**

Now what the hell do we do? Well, one of the first things is think about a name. Which can be as complicated or as simple as you allow it to be. In the end, it comes down to what feels right. And compromise… of course.

We throw around a couple of names in Florida. *The big book of 60,000 baby names* is overwhelming though, and I don't see one decent name that I like. Achilles, Thor, Entilades. Really? Come on. There's nothing 'reasonable' that I haven't already considered.

It's more than just a daft book though, it's one of those things that you do to get excited about it all.

Never before in my life did I ever have the need, desire nor inclination to buy a book like that. I like to think that I'm a reasonably sensible fella. I know these things have been created with the sole purpose of extracting money from saps like me about to have a kid. And, sap that I am, I buy it.

I did try and keep an eye on that sort of shit though. I should know better. I work in marketing and I know that the best customer in the world is a first-time pregnant mum.

When you go into a baby shop you realise there's an entire industry built on it. But wait, I'm getting ahead of myself.

Baby names. I read through the author's tips on the first things to consider. It's not very useful. Just choose a name. It should be quite simple, shouldn't it? Hmm. That being said, we were about half way through the pregnancy before we reached a consensus.

We have to think about boys' and girls' names of course. 'Foetus' isn't really a very nice term, and we end up using 'peanut' in the meantime; 'it' just sounds rude. Even still, peanut needs a gender. My reference always seems to be 'the wee fella', 'the wee man', or 'him'.

A healthy little baby is all you want, really, but I can't deny a leaning towards having a boy. I have this vague picture of teaching him rugby, football, how to ski. Then again a girl would just mean these things shift a little, more skiing, tennis and sailing, less football and rugby. Not so bad really.

With girls it's the other stuff, when they get a bit older that I wouldn't be too keen on, like the boyfriends. Not too sure how I would deal with that sort of palaver. I gave my sister's boyfriends a terribly hard time when we were growing up, and I'm awfully protective of any females I'm close to. I think Erin would have to tie me up not to kill somebody who messed my daughter around.

I'll be over the moon with whatever happens I'm sure. But my tendency towards a boy eventually prompts Erin to suggest that we find out what sex the kid is. I'm not so sure about that. I think it's nice to leave that bit of surprise. Erin reckons I'll get such a shock if a girl pops out however, that we need to find out in advance—give me time to get used to the idea.

In the end however, just like telling Fraser and Jane about the pregnancy, circumstances end up making the decision for us.

We get back to Sydney and life moves pretty fast. We have friends staying and we've got a wedding to go to in Melbourne, so it's busy, busy, busy. Erin decides to not go to Melbourne but insists I do. "Enjoy the trip, I'll be fine and it's only a couple of days," she says. But what's really going on is a little more complicated.

One evening in Costa Rica, Erin woke up with a pain in her stomach. She had never felt anything like it before and was more than a little distressed, of course, because she was pregnant. It goes away pretty quickly, but returns on the night I fly to Melbourne, so she books herself in for the first available scan - the following day.

I check into my hotel room and call Erin as I'm on the way to meet the wedding crew. She tells me what's happening and tries to hold back the tears, but eventually they burst through, and I feel like the worst person in the world for not being there. She's afraid that all is not going according to nature's plan. The pain has come back and she doesn't feel good at all.

I decide to fly home the next day but Erin talks me into staying. Telling me she really is fine; just tired and emotional. The next evening I can't face another night out with everyone, so I have dinner in a little Italian restaurant with my friends Sandy, Zoe and their kids who are over from Scotland.

Erin calls towards the end of the meal and tells me all is going to be well—she's been scanned, the baby has a heartbeat, and the pain looks as if it had been coming from a cyst, which was going to have no adverse affect on the wee fella at all. Woo hoo! The relief is overwhelming, and it's great to hear the comfort in Erin's voice. Brilliant!

Although it's early days I can't contain myself, I tell Sandy and Zoe and they're very happy for us. We finish the evening off by walking along the pier at St Kilda and watching the penguins at the end, a takeaway coffee and a slow stroll home. It's a lovely evening. I get to spend some quality time with some of my best friends in the world, and I find out that all is well with Erin. Can't ask for much more than that.

The weather is beautiful for the wedding the next day, and after the service in the Botanical Gardens we all head off to a venue in Docklands. Surprise, surprise, I get thrown out. Well I was out already. It's just that I'm not let back in. I was taking a pee off the pier, a fairly common activity for a Scotsman in a kilt I might add, however one of the bouncers takes exception to it.

A little harsh I think so I make my feelings known, and after arguing for a while I realise they're serious, so I let them know exactly what I think of them. And that seals the deal. Fuckers. I'm not so sure I'm fatherhood material really.

I'm supposed to stay another night in Melbourne after the wedding, but I feel an overwhelming urge to get back to Sydney. I change my flight and head home the next morning. I don't tell Erin I'm coming back early so she is surprised, but pleased to see me. And it has never felt so good to see her.

Eventually, life finally slows down. We have an evening and the whole of Sunday to relax, take it easy and catch our breath. Just perfect. Just what we need.

That waiting period though, not knowing, trying not to fear the worst. Then waiting to hear the results of the scan. All of that was just awful. So, partly as a result of the experience, we decide to wait until the 12-week scan before telling anybody else about the pregnancy.

I don't even allow myself to think about it. Well, let's say I don't allow the thoughts to kick around for too long. We hardly talk about it, and we stop discussing names. You don't want to get your hopes up, then find out that it's a no go.

And so begins a long period of *not* discussing the peanut.

During Erin's visit to the Sydney Ultrasound Clinic for Women, she'd picked up a book that provided a week-by-week update of the baby's, and the mother's progress.

Every Saturday we read the relevant section, and that's all we allow ourselves. A brief chat and that's it. Until the 12-week scan that is.

We decide that one book is enough for the information we need. No need to overload. That's the intention anyway. People just threw them at us when they heard a baby was on the way though. Overall it's a weird time, plodding along in limbo and not discussing what is never too far from the front of my mind—even with the person I'm closest to in the world.

Despite our *supposed* embargo on the baby talk, Erin somehow discovers that her best friend in Ireland has also fallen pregnant, and is only a week behind us. Don't know how they figured that out if we're not supposed to be telling anyone—but hey. There are many long discussions with Catherine, and because she's a radiographer who specialises in ultrasound, she knows all sorts about the process. I soon discover however, being aware of everything that can go wrong with a pregnancy is not necessarily a good thing. Erin has occasional bouts of doubt and worry, which in turn rub off on me.

Eventually I realise we have to be careful who we listen to. We have to let nature take its course and if it works out great, if not, then at least we know Erin can actually get pregnant. So many people just can't, or go through years of trying. We try and remind ourselves how lucky we are.

Our good friend Sophie is a great help. Erin met her years ago in Sydney, they kept in touch and we lived with Sophie when we first arrived in Australia. She's also a radiographer, a naturopath and all round hippy. She's really positive and having been a birth partner already, knows a lot more about childbirth than we do. She helps keep the worries in check which at this point in the proceedings, is exactly what we need.

Time did fly during that period though, and it hasn't exactly slowed down yet.

I remember hearing Billy Connolly talking about a whole year going by in just a flash. "Christmas, New year, your birthday and, fuck me, it's Christmas again!" Now I know how you feel Billy. I suspect it's more to do with age than the pregnancy situation. Anyhoo, time flew; still does.

With all this going on in the background, I find it difficult to get too stressed out about anything work related. Life's general annoyances appear rather small when faced with the possibility of having or not having a wee baby. And that certainly helps with the fact that my job is touch and go.

Then we find out that another good friend has a brain aneurysm, and once again, perspective helps us handle our own concerns. So what if I lose my job, I'll just get another one, it's not the end of the world. Then the Haiti earthquake hits. Shit. Even more perspective. Poor buggers.

I guess what I learned was to never to take the situation for granted, and to try and appreciate every stage. Leave the worrying until there's actually something to be worried about. Of course, that's easier said than done.

Nesting instinct?
Is there such a thing as the nesting instinct? Until recently I would probably have said no, what a load of crap. However, not long after we get back from our US trip, I find myself reorganising all my cupboards and clothes.

It didn't seem that long ago that my laundry 'basket' was an entire corner of the room. I had a mattress on the floor, breezeblocks and a couple of wooden planks for shelves. Reorganising back then would have meant moving the skis into the hallway so I didn't trip on them. Single man back then though.

Roll on twenty years and I have an unexpected and genuine desire to tidy up and organise. Even when everything is in order, Erin and I find ourselves frantically hanging pictures that have been lying around since we moved in, shifting furniture, going to the DIY store for bits and pieces. Most unusual behaviour.

It's not even a one off, it's consistent, and we're happy doing this for about three or four weekends in a row. Even more surprising, I *keep* everything in order afterwards. Thankfully I snap out of it eventually and take myself off for a number of beers.

Nesting instinct? Or just common sense… Maybe an awareness that the time to do all this stuff is running out? Maybe the knowledge that if I'm going to be spending a lot more time at home, I might as well make it as comfortable as possible?

I guess that's what instinct is, common sense and foresight, allowing you to prepare for future events.

Anyway, nesting, or whatever, is doing funny things to me.

Years ago I saw a Gandhi quote in a window in Zanzibar. I read it, walked on then stopped. Turned around and wrote it down on an old envelope I happened to have.

As I traveled across Africa, back home, out to the States and eventually down to the Caribbean, the envelope gathered other little pieces of wisdom, observations and mementos. When I moved to Australia it came with me too, and during my month of organisation, of picture hanging and nesting, I find I have to lay my hands on it.

I want to frame it and hang it somewhere. It becomes a minor obsession and, when I can't find it I panic, searching everywhere in the house until it turns up in a drawer. The relief is huge, and I realise the level of anxiety I'm feeling is inconsistent with what I'm actually looking for. I know it's just a bit of paper; I know I could look the quote up, but I really need to unearth this tattered little relic of my past.

> *"To me life is far too great a mystery, far too sacred a gift of God to be praised adequately from one particular angle. And that is why I said so categorically that the greatest artist is he who lives the finest life. Yesterday is gone, tomorrow has not yet come, but today is ours, to make or mar. Let us fill it with small deeds nobly done. But noble deeds come from noble thoughts."*—Mahatma Gandhi

I believe this to be 100 percent correct. *That* is how people should live their lives. And I suppose it reinforces this new step in mine, as being just another one of life's experiences. Growth. Viewing things from as many different perspectives as possible. Words of wisdom from a great man, discovered by a younger me.

Perhaps I don't want life's events to overtake me, and maybe it is a reminder of my idealistic self. Someone I want to hold on to. Who knows.

Anyway, it's framed now and sits on my desk. I read it often.

7

The First Scan

"We do not remember days, we remember moments."
—Cesare Pavese. **Amen to that.**

An old man is lying in a hospital bed, talking about how all the big moments in life are behind him. Falling in love, getting married, having children and seeing them grow up. All the little things that go with these landmarks of life, all behind him. What does he have left to look forward to? Although it's only a TV show, the thought is more than a little bit sad. I seem to be having a lot of these moments now, they're coming thick and fast. It's exciting, relentless.

The first scan is one of those moments. It's actually the second scan, but it's my first. I duck out of work saying I have to see the doctor about my neck, and twenty minutes later I'm in a totally different world full of nurses, pregnant women and gossip magazines. They know how to keep you waiting in there too, and they force you to read those magazines.

Eventually we're called through to the ultrasound area, which has a bed and a massive flat-screen opposite. The perfect place to spend an afternoon watching movies.

There's a Star Trek console to one side, and a seat for me on the other. All three of us take our positions and before you know it, up goes the skirt. A jelly is applied to the belly and within seconds, an image appears on the screen. I've seen this sort of thing on TV before so it's not a total surprise, however there's nothing recognisable at first. The radiographer knows what she's looking for though. She maneuvers the instrument until suddenly, there it is. That's my wee boy up there, my wee girl. Totally amazing.

That was the moment, that was the whole world right there. While the afterglow remained for the rest of the day, for maybe five minutes in there - it was almost overwhelming. Even now writing about it, I'm welling up.

I almost cry but manage to hold it in. The radiographer asks a doctor to look at the cyst discovered in the last scan, and we're assured there is nothing to worry about. Off you go, see you in a few weeks.

We leave on a wave of relief. Erin seems to be finally putting her demons to rest, with negative thoughts and doubts replaced by reassuring fact. At freakin' last.

We allow ourselves a day of being excited again, then it is back to holding it all in. Meanwhile I've designed the kid's room in my head. I've painted an 'Under the sea' mural in my imagination, but that's as far as it is allowed to go.

Although it's a milestone we aren't out of the woods just yet. In between *Hello* magazines, I managed to read a few leaflets about the nuchal translucency test—the 12-week scan I've heard so much about. When you can reliably call yourself pregnant. This is the first time I'd read anything in detail about it though.

Weekly stages: The facts
Pregnancy is all about the weeks. 38 of them to be exact. Your doctor will, however, be talking about 40 weeks—which

includes the two weeks of preparation before conception. There's quite a lot happening in these two weeks. The shedding of the uterus (menstruation), the egg beginning its journey (ovulation), the egg and the sperm meeting (fertilisation) and then, finally, the egg implanting in the uterus wall (conception). The average normal pregnancy is 283 days, or 40 weeks and three days, and is further divided into trimesters.

The first is Week 1 to 13 (a likely period for morning sickness); second trimester runs from Week 14 to 26 (also known as the honeymoon period), and the third trimester, Weeks 27 to 40 (the final countdown).

Our 12-week scan
The nuchal translucency test provides the odds of your child having a series of genetic diseases, one of which is Down syndrome. The other couple of diseases I can pretty much guarantee you've never heard of before, but basically they mean your child will have a couple of years to live, if it isn't stillborn. Just about the most horrible thing you could possibly imagine.

Needless to say this is the big one. If you make it past the 12-week scan with the all clear, the chance of miscarriage reduces to something like 2 percent. Twenty percent of all pregnancies end up in miscarriage. Approximately eighty percent in the first trimester. That's for all women, not just women who are a bit older. The chances jump significantly when a woman is over 35, as Erin is now.

So before the test we have a conversation. What do we do if they tell us we're going to have a child with Down syndrome? I guess you never know the answer to that until you're realistically faced with it. We both feel the same fortunately. We'd go for it anyway, so at least we're prepared whatever the outcome.

They take us into the room pretty quickly this time. The wee guy has grown amazingly since the last scan only a few weeks ago, and according to the radiographer everything seems to be in order. She even uses the word 'perfect' a couple of times. I'm sure she says this to lots of people, but I actually feel proud of the wee fella. So all looks good, but what we're really here for is the results of the nucal test.

It's not a simple yes or no you get here. They take a number of factors into consideration (age, weight, blood tests and the results of the previous scans) and then give you the odds of your child having a genetic disorder.

Before heading in, we thought that with Erin's age, 1 in 300 for Down syndrome was to be expected. If it got down to 1 in 200 we would consider the next test. Which is more invasive and carries a bit of risk, but gives us a definitive answer. Then again maybe we wouldn't bother, as we've decided to go ahead anyway.

So, back into the waiting room where we sit for about three weeks. It's really only forty minutes, but it's quite possibly the longest wait of my life. Time is most certainly relative. Eventually, "McLeod". We go through to the doctor's room and it's a nice corner office, so we're sitting with a top doc—good.

The result? 1 in 5,200 chance of Down syndrome. The other disorders—1 in 50,000 or something like that. I'm stunned into silence. The doctor asks if I am alright, and I stumble into talk mode.

"Ay yeah." I repeat what I've just been told, ask for confirmation, get the answer I know is coming, and here it is—another moment. Phwooo. This one lasts much longer.

It's like a drug. If I left on a wave of relief before, this time I'm flying. So happy. I can't wipe the smile off my face. This is it, it's real, it's happening now. At last, after all this time of holding it all in, it can finally come flooding out. Yee fucking hah!

For Erin it's the same—excitement and huge relief, probably more so than we're both expecting. I guess both of us are not quite cognisant of the fact that we've been holding our emotions in check so much. But here we are, full steam ahead.

We get in the car and I flick around the radio stations. It lands on 'Under the sea' from the Little Mermaid, in Spanish right enough, but still… I can't believe it. The mural comes a little closer to reality. I'm not going back to work this time, and we end up sitting in a little coffee shop close to home. We order coffees and a celebratory piece of cheesecake. Woo hoo! It's nice having an afternoon off.

Some days, on my way to meetings or whatever, I often see people sitting in the park, or in coffee shops. Not just at lunchtime, but at 3 or 4 o'clock in the afternoon. When you're caught up in that world of work it seems impossible to imagine what these people could be up to. With older folks, or mothers with kids, that's fair enough—but people like me, blokes who're too old to be studying and not old enough to retire. What the hell are they up to?

Sitting here now, it occurs to me I'm one of those guys. I have an answer. You never do know what people are up to. As much as you might surmise a reason for a mid-30s guy to be sitting nonchalantly in a coffee shop on a Thursday afternoon, you would never guess that he's not alone, his wife has gone to the toilet and he's just found out that he's 100 percent going to be a father. No chance. Even with the quirky grin on his face.

You never bloody know.

Apart from 'Under the sea' on the radio, there's another coincidence too. We're told the due date is 5 September; which is the day I arrived in Colorado back in 1995. The very beginning of my travels, and with this new wee person about to herald in the start of another great adventure, it seems quite fitting.

12-week scan: The facts
The first trimester finishes at the end of the thirteenth week, but it's the 12-week stage that's more significant.

An ultrasound during the twelfth week measures the soft tissue, or fluid thickness on the back of the baby's neck—known as the nuchal translucency. A larger nuchal translucency indicates a greater chance of Down syndrome, and this, combined with the mother's age, and the levels of a couple of proteins give you the odds of your child having Down syndrome.

Only 5 percent of all pregnancies at this stage end up falling into the 'high risk of Downs' category—'more than 1 in 300' chance. So even then, the risks are slim.

At 12 weeks a baby is only 5.6cm long, but has developed a tremendous amount already, only needing to grow from this point on. Here's what's been happening in the build up to this crucial point in time.

Week 1—Menstruation. The shedding of the lining of the womb, which is kind of like ploughing the field. The uterus is then ready to build up the lining again, in preparation for a fertilised egg to be planted.

Week 2—Although men create millions of sperm every day, women are limited to the eggs they are born with. The eggs grow older as she does and, with age, the division process that one of them is about to undertake (meiosis) becomes more and more difficult. Meiosis begins at the start of the second week. The 46 chromosomes inside one of the eggs duplicate, and then divide into four sets of 23 pairs. Only one of these sets will partner up with another 23 pairs delivered by the successful sperm—creating a baby with the combined genetic material of its mother and father.

Healthy conception becomes more difficult with age, because the energy levels stored in the eggs depletes over time, and with less energy to complete the complicated process of meiosis, there's more of a chance of something going wrong. An extra chromosome sneaking through in pair 21 for example, is Down syndrome.

Increased levels of oestrogen and progesterone are produced at this time too, hormones that instruct the uterus to thicken.

Week 3—This is it! The egg is heading down the fallopian tube and the sperm are swimming fervently up in the opposite direction. It can take a couple of days for them to hook up, so the launch date might not be the date of fertilisation. When they do meet the sperm burrows into the egg, their chromosomes intermingle and hey presto, you're off and running. The embryo develops into a ball of cells, and enters the uterine cavity on the fourth day after fertilisation. It floats around for another couple of days, then implants into the uterine wall around day 6–12. That's the big moment. Conception. Two out of every three conceptions will miscarry, many without a woman even knowing about it. Once the pregnancy is confirmed however, there's an 85 percent chance of making it to birth.

Week 4—The placenta begins to grow, and plants its roots into the uterus seeking to connect with the circulatory system. Until the connection is established the embryo draws its sustenance from the wall of the uterus. It's officially called a blastocyst right now, and will soon develop into an embryonic disc. It's about now that pregnancy tests are able to detect increased levels of HCG (human chorionic gonadotropin).

Week 5—A woman's 'embryonic disc' will be visible on ultrasound towards the end of this week and it's even possible to see and hear a heartbeat (another indication that the pregnancy is going according to plan). If you reach this stage the chance of miscarriage drops yet again. Ninety percent of babies with a heartbeat in Week 5 make it all the way. The baby is large enough that it can be measured fairly accurately now too, and this allows you to determine its age (to within 3 days). If a mother is going to suffer morning sickness it can start any time now, and doesn't necessarily have to be in the morning either.

Week 6—Getting bigger now, and the heartbeat of the baby quickens considerably, up from 60 to about 100bmp. Both ends of the spine close over, its development now complete.

Week 7—Future bundles of joy are now 1cm long. The baby's heart rate is up to 140 bpm and the placenta takes over in providing life support and room service for the little one. You'll be taking over these duties, for the rest of your life, soon enough.

Week 8—Baby's head can actually be recognised as that of a human being as opposed to a kidney bean for the first time. Limb 'buds' can be seen, and many of the organs are reaching their final stages of development. The heart is going like the clappers, registering 160 bpm—like an adult at full sprint. Mothers tend to be pretty exhausted by Week 8 and the advice: 'Don't' stand when you can sit, don't sit when you can lie down', should be taken seriously.

Week 9—The heart reaches 180bpm, which is the fastest a resting heart will ever go, and after this week it begins to slow down again, returning to 140bpm by birth. Arms and legs are now more obvious, and can be seen with an ultrasound to be moving around. At 2.4cm from head to toe—your kid is almost fully developed by just this ninth week. Amazing. Less than three months to build the most sophisticated being on the planet. I can't even read a book in three months anymore.

Week 10—You're down to only a 2–3 percent chance of miscarriage now, and the proportions of the baby become more recognisable, less like something out of a David Lynch movie.

Week11—Junior is 4.4cm in length, might be asleep on the odd occasion and can be woken with a cough. HCG is at its peak, and as the levels begin to reduce from here on, morning sickness fades.

Week 12—5.6cm. A small nuchal translucency indicates low risk of heart and genetic problems. 95 percent of all babies at this stage are found to be low risk of having Down syndrome.

The other thing that 12 weeks means? Tell the world!

8

Woo Hoo! Tell The World...

"Oh life is going to change now!"
—Harry MacLeod. **Oh how true.**

Now of course we can tell people all about it. Explain why Erin has been the designated driver for a while, let it all out!

I'm not in the mood to tell anyone though. Maybe it's a come down from caffeine, sugar and adrenaline, but I don't feel very well. We get home, settle in for the night and I think—hmm, what now?

Erin tries to call her mum and can't get through, so she speaks to one of her sisters while I sit on my own, pondering.

Maybe I'm experiencing some sort of delayed reaction. I don't know but I'm starting to freak out a little bit. I keep it to myself and it's gone after a couple of hours. I think the gravity of the situation is beginning to sink in. The whole process is indeed filled with highs and lows, periods of don't know and what the fuck, joy and delight, then shitting yourself, for any number of reasons.

Anyway I just can't face calling, I want to be in a good mood when telling my sister and my dad about it, and it just isn't the night for it.

I call my sister the next day on the drive to work—I can usually get a quick 10 minutes to the UK at that time of the morning. She's in the pub with a couple of friends when I tell her, and she is delighted for us.

I get dad later on that evening and he's happy for us too. "That's great son" he laughs "Oh life is going to change now, Iain. Oh ho ho."

No shit, although at that point in time I had no idea by how much.

He goes on to say he had an inkling I was going to tell him that. My friend Patrick says the same when I tell him a couple of nights later, and I know the feeling myself. I've experienced it when people have told me—sometimes you just know what they're going to say. I guess around this age though, having been married for a year or two it doesn't take a genius to figure out what big news there might be.

It is great to be openly excited at last, having bottled it up for so long. It seems that little bit closer to reality, and now the genie's out I start doing some research in the most dangerous place on the planet—the Internet.

A place where opinion is served as fact, facts are diluted and dispersed with opinion, and only the brave would base their most important decisions on. Ha!

That being said, I think I managed to extract some reasonably enlightening information about the road ahead. In regards to this whole baby thing – it looks as if we may, in fact, be the victims of our own success, in evolutionary terms that is.

Evolution and babies: The facts

One of the main concerns about having a baby, is the fact that they're so bloody useless. So unable to do anything for themselves that you, as parents, become subjugated to their every whim, burp, fart, cry and shitty nappy. For the most advanced species on the planet it doesn't seem like a very efficient arrangement. And that's because it's not, but it hasn't always been like this.

Let's go back a few million years. Humans didn't exist but our predecessors were around, swinging from tree to tree and having a fine old time.

For what is believed to be climatic reasons, we eventually came down from the trees in order to forage for food—and on land it was easier to get around on two legs, as opposed to four. So we evolved, stood upright and, along with the move to ground level, started eating more meat. This is generally considered a key factor in our becoming a more intelligent species. I eat a lot of meat myself.

Two legs changed the distribution of weight on our bodies however, and in order to deal with the new stresses and strains, we had to adapt. The pelvis thickened and strengthened, and in women this, unfortunately, narrowed the birth canal. This alone might not have presented a problem, but when combined with our bigger brains—caused by our increasing levels of intelligence—well nature did the only thing it could do. If a fully developed baby's head was now too big to fit through the birth canal, the baby would just have to make the journey before it was fully developed.

This is called the obstetrical dilemma hypothesis and although it makes sense, it also makes for a pretty intensive parenting experience.

Studies have recently emerged to challenge the obstetrical dilemma hypothesis, suggesting it could be the mother's metabolic rate that is more significant than the size of the head. A new theory contends that by nine-months a baby's demands for energy exceed the mother's ability to generate enough to keep them both going. So the eject button is pushed.

Another idea proposed in the 60s indicates that babies being born before their brains are fully developed, ensures they are 'outside' so they can soak up all of the cultural influences that exist in our very social world.

I'm not a scientist, but my money is on the obstetrical dilemma. And although it's all very interesting, it's of no practical help in dealing with the 'extreme parenting' that we seem to have ended up with. That said, exploring the theory does help me understand the 'why' of what I'm about to get into, if not the 'how on earth' am I going to deal with it.

9

A Wandering Mind

"He was swimming in a sea of other people's expectations. Men had drowned in seas like that."
—Robert Jordan. **Aye, you gotta watch that.**

After a quick spate of telling people our news, things settle down. Back to a normal life and there are no more appointments until the next scan, six weeks away. Erin isn't showing a bump, and we still read our book every week telling us what's going on. I buy my painting gear for the nursery, although it's a while before I start painting anything, and that's our life for a while.

Except of course, at the back of my mind I'm still doing this dance between terror and delight. Contentment most of the time though I must admit. And although there's a bit of a break in the proceedings, there's plenty to think about.

How much is it all going to cost anyway? Private or public hospital? Babies freaking everywhere! This part is actually quite unbelievable. Of course they've always been there. Pregnant women too. But, how the hell didn't I notice them before? I must have been blind, there really are an awful lot of them. Even on TV, someone's having a kid, someone's just found out they're a dad, there's a whole show just about someone who's about to have a kid! What the fuck?

I tell my financial advisor—Tony—that we've passed the 12-week stage and he's effusive about being a parent. He's got three kids and loves every minute of it. His best advice—get a comfy chair, and put your name down for a childcare centre, now.

We discuss the financial implications. It looks like Erin will stop work for 9 months, only three of which are paid. I've started a spreadsheet to see how we can manage, and what the expected costs might be. He tells me not to bother, it costs what it costs, it costs a lot, you just muddle through. I was thinking about stopping anyway, it was too frightening. Yet it is difficult not to worry, even just a little bit about the money situation.

Fortunately we've worked our asses off for some time now, and we do have a healthy buffer of cash but it took so long to build up it would be heartbreaking to see all that money just peter away. Anyway, that's what it's for I suppose.

Tony, funnily enough is one of the few people who says it's the best thing you can do, it's brilliant, you'll love it. Yeah you'll be tired, but it's so worth it. It's nice to hear.

The private or public decision I leave up to Erin. Being a radiographer she knows so much more about the whole medical set-up than I do. We end up doing a bit of a mix. Private for the first few scans and then we jump to public—and so far that's been fantastic, so we'll stick with that. Should anything veer off the straight and narrow, we're off to private again. For example, Erin's placenta is low and if it doesn't move up she'll need a caesarian. That's where we'd jump ship to private. Sounds like a plan.

It is quite a shift, internally, once you've told everybody what's going on.

It's a journey even just to get to this stage. We'd made the decision, succeeded in getting pregnant, held our breath through the first 12 weeks, then at last… phew, exhale, tell everyone.

Now with the waiting game over my mind can wander a little, and that's not always a good thing. There are all sorts of expectations floating around in relation to this father and provider deal. Of course I want to shield them financially from anything untoward, and there's the expectation of providing not just a safe, but also a nice home for my family. I find myself in danger of piling all of them up on my shoulders.

It's a hefty burden for someone with a bit of an adventurous spirit, someone who likes to up and leave at the drop of a hat or, for example, would like to sail around the world one day.

I'm not normally one for bowing to expectations, but I've never been 'almost' a father before. Sometimes it's difficult to know what the hell's going on.

What was going on?
Although all of this was understandably causing a fair amount of stress, there was something else going on that I couldn't put my finger on. Sure the GFC had hit, and jobs everywhere were a little shaky, but the lack of security wasn't an issue.

Looking back, I think I was lonely. I know it sounds stupid. I was so happy with Erin and the fact that we were about to become parents. Apart from Erin though, I had nobody I felt I could talk to about it. I became quite homesick, and I felt an insipid, unwelcome pressure in my chest.

I felt my friends were drifting away, soon to become non-existent. I wasn't into going to the pub so much anymore, and that's just about all they seemed to do. And with family on the other side of the world, when normally they'd be around more than ever to help you both through the impending change, it was pretty isolating.

One night after Erin had gone to bed—about 8pm on a Saturday night—I called round to see our friends and neighbours, Tamar and Jules. They're lovely folks who had twins a couple of years ago. We had a couple of bottles of wine and I talked non-stop about what was happening.

They managed to squeeze in a word or two, when I paused to throw another glass of wine down my gullet, but they didn't get much of a chance. I hadn't realised how much I needed to get all this stuff out. And despite a little hangover the next day, I felt so much better for just having talked to someone about everything that was going on.

They listened to me well that night, and I think that was all I was in need of. Just to get it all out, the questions, the concerns, the comical bits-—lubricated by a couple of bottles of wine of course. Cathartic, purging drunkenness.

Tamar mentioned one thing that really stuck with me too, and I guess, comforted me a little in the face of the great unknown. "All babies need is love, warmth and food." In retrospect, it wasn't too far from the truth.

What I know, now, is that it's really important to talk about it all. Have a few beers now and again, talk to other dads, talk to other guys in the same situation. I don't think I did enough of that, and I think it would have been easier if I had.

Also while I'm doling out the advice, I'd say it's a good idea to know what's going on from a medical perspective too. The more you know the more involved you are in the whole process, which just makes it all the more enjoyable. It is a joint venture after all. I probably shirked my duties on that front a little bit.

18-Week scan

You know how every now and again, there's a day, a week, or a short period of time where absolutely everything happens at once? Well for me, that's the 18-week scan.

Within one 24-hour period I get drunk, embarrass myself, get made redundant and find out that the wee one is A-OK. Quite a day. Quite a week actually.

It's Wednesday night and I head into town after work to catch up with a couple of guys I haven't seen in a long time. I guess I'm drifting away from most of my friends, none of whom are in a similar position to me - looking down the barrel of parenthood.

I don't go to the pub so much anymore, and the result of trying to keep up with regular pub goers? Legless. Of course. Not only do I come home drunk and annoy my pregnant wife, but I lose my suit jacket and my workbag to boot. What a freakin' idiot. I get home early however—11pm, so I wake up the next day without too much of a hangover, just a little tired. The main pain I'm feeling however, is self-imposed embarrassment, and disappointment.

I have the morning off so Erin and I can go to the 18-week scan, and as we head off to the clinic we're not exactly on the best of terms.

The radiographer asks if we'd like to know if the child is a boy or a girl, and we still haven't made our minds up yet. We were supposed to have discussed it this morning, but since we're not talking to each other, we ask if it's possible for her to write it down, and put it in an envelope for us to open up and read later (maybe). She says she's not allowed.

Can you believe that? I'm guessing in case it's wrong, so there's no possibility of returning later, with thousands of dollars worth of pink clothes and a kid called Tom, and suing them. What a nonsense. So once again the decision makes itself. I think it's a good one though, and in the end it doesn't really matter.

The scan shows all is progressing well and there are no abnormalities. Great. We have a quick bite to eat, I drop Erin off at work and then call the pub to see if they have my bag. They do. Thank god for that. I drive straight over to pick it up, and they have my suit jacket too, fantastic! I take all of this as an indication of good luck. All is going to be well.

I'd ruined the experience of the 18-week scan, but the recovery of my bag and jacket makes me feel I'm back on track.

I walk into work apologising for the length of time it took at the hospital. I walk over to my boss and say "I promised myself I wasn't going to become one of those people, but I don't care—I am." I show him a picture of the peanut, then wander over to my colleague.

"I'm afraid I might have to bore you to tears with this baby stuff for a while now, Leesa."

"Well that's your job Iain, I'll let you know when I've had enough," she says.

I'm quite emotional and have to excuse myself to make a coffee. My good friend and colleague, Adrianne, comes in from lunch and I show her the pictures. Then my boss asks if he can have a word with me downstairs, and he fires me, gives me the flick, lets me go, or, whatever the fuck you want to call it. Fuck.

It wasn't completely out of the blue; the company was going through a rough patch with the GFC. Adrianne and I had been joking for ages about who'd be first to go. But it was still a shock—especially on that day. Big fallout with Erin, feeling shit about myself, great result from the 18-week scan, getting my bag and jacket back, feeling as if things were turning back in my favour, and then getting the heave ho. Highs and lows, indeed.

Erin calls as we're winding everything up and I quickly tell her what's happened. She relays this information to Sophie, who later joins me at home with a care package of sushi, crisps and dips. Good ol' Sophie.

Just another day on the road to fatherhood.

It takes me about a week to slow down, stop waking up thinking about work and things that need to be done. I don't think I realised how much stress I was under until it all fell apart. I take that week to de-stress, get back to normal, catch up on the myriad of things in life that never seem to get done when you're working.

I don't even want to think about looking for another job for a good while either. And when I do get around to it, one thing I've decided for sure—whatever I do next it has to give me more time at home with Erin and the little one, and is hopefully a lot less stressful.

18-week scan: The facts

Week 13— This is the last week of the first trimester, and a lot of things start happening. Your baby becomes waterproof for a start. The skin becomes 'keratinised' which helps maintain the barrier against the fluid in the amniotic cavity. Their kidneys begin to work, cleaning the blood and extracting the waste.

The heart rate has slowed to 160bmp. The arms and legs are moving independently, and the chest can be seen moving up and down—'breathing' in the amniotic fluid. This helps exercise the chest muscles and is important for the development of the lungs. The placenta takes over as the single source of oxygen and nutrients for the baby, and although the kidneys are doing their job, the umbilical cord still carries some of the waste away through the placenta, into the mother's blood stream for disposal.

Week 14— The beginning of the 'honeymoon phase' of the pregnancy, the second trimester. When a pregnant woman is said to be glowing—it's about now. Generally a woman's hair will be thicker and shinier, her skin clear and radiant. This is a busy week for your baby too. Starting at the top, hair begins to grow on its head and eyebrows take sprout. Eyelids are formed. Your baby's eyes are moving closer together, and the ears are moving up the side of the head.

They can now swallow. The head has moved up and away from the chest, and you can see that they actually have a neck. Fingernails are growing, and fingerprints begin to take shape. Muscles are also beginning to form over the developing joints—which results in a lot more movement. They'll be moving hundreds of times a day although your partner probably won't feel it yet. Toenails form, and a downy kind of hair that protects the skin, called lanugo, begins to grow all over the body. It disappears a couple of weeks before birth.

Inside the baby, the thyroid has matured to the stage where it's now producing hormones. In boys, the prostate takes shape, in girls the ovaries are beginning to descend from high up in the abdomen to enter the pelvis. The kidneys start making urine and it's expelled into the amniotic cavity. Finally, blood begins to form in the bone marrow.

There's a lot going on and in addition to all of this, a baby will have grown to about 7–9cm. There's now less than 2 percent chance of a miscarriage.

Week 15—Hormones will be playing havoc in most women by now, an emotionally draining experience for all. The baby continues to grow at a furious pace however.

The hair continues to grow. Face muscles are formed, contracting involuntarily making frowns and raising eyebrows in apparent surprise. Fists are clenched and unclenched, feet are pointing, and the ears have almost moved all the way up into place.

The bone marrow continues to develop, producing blood that can now be seen coursing through the blood vessels beneath the skin. The skeleton is getting harder too, although it needs to retain a certain amount of flexibility in order to make it out of the birth canal. Chances are this is the first time you'll be able to tell the sex of your baby, if you want to find out that is.

Week 16—Your baby begins to take control for the first time. The nervous system has developed to such an extent that those involuntary muscle contractions, now become voluntary. It's the first sign of consciousness, and what they tend to do with their new found power—is kick their legs even more, and make little grasping movements with their hands. They begin to hiccup, as a precursor to breathing and their eyes are now sensitive to light—although it's pitch black where they are right now.

In females, millions of eggs begin to form inside the ovaries. Even before they're born however, they die off—leaving just a million at birth. By the time the first period arrives, it's down to half a million, and the eggs continue dying all the way through to menopause. By that stage only about 400 eggs will have matured and ovulated, providing the opportunity for the process to begin all over again. Baby is 11–12 cm, and weighs 70–95gms.

Week 17—The circulatory and urinary systems are now operating perfectly, and the baby will form what's called 'brown fat', to help keep them warm after birth.

Week 18—The ridiculous growth spurt the baby has been undergoing for the last five weeks begins to slow down. In addition to the ability to control their own muscles, they now have taste buds and will begin sucking their thumb. If it's a girl, there are as many as six million eggs in the ovaries. Any abnormalities in the heart can be detected by ultrasound.

The inner ear bones have grown, and the baby can hear for the first time. What they hear is blood coursing through the umbilical cord, and their mother's heartbeat. Loud noises are likely to startle them, and the placenta is now as big as the baby.

10

Last Chance Saloon

"A father is someone who carries photos of their children in their wallet where their money used to be."
—Unknown. **I can believe that.**

Meanwhile, outside in the real world Erin and I begin to realise it's last chance saloon for a number of things. I've been threatening to organise a mini golf tournament for at least a year, and I don't mean windmills and crocodiles, I mean eight or so guys playing a wee tournament one Saturday afternoon, followed by a few beers. It's even written down in a list of 'things I'm going to do this year—2009'. I'm finally getting around to it in the first half of 2010, so that's not so bad.

I'm sure it's prompted by the knowledge that 'outings' like that are going to be a bit more difficult when a baby arrives, so I finally get off my ass and get on with it. I send an email round, and soon I'm questioning why I've been so hesitant. Turns out, it's a doddle. The response is immediate and within two days I have eight booked onto a local course for a tournament.

It's a great day. Quite a few of the blokes have kids, and I think they enjoy just spending time away from the world of domesticity. Talking shit, playing golf and having a laugh.

We have a couple of beers afterwards and there is enthusiastic talk about when the next one is going to be.

We also decide to have a few trips before the little one arrives. Erin's sister, Niamh, joins us on a flight up to Brisbane for the Anzac holiday weekend, and my newfound open mind and fascination with the iPhone comes back to bite me in the ass, or the ankle, as it were.

I'm walking down a set of stairs by the waterfront, and I don't see the missing brick because I have my head in my iPhone.

I've literally just said how amazing Google Maps is, when the real world strikes and fractures my freakin' ankle. Fucking technology. Fucking open-minded bollocks.

It's good timing of course because I have no job right now, and I'm getting into lots of running and fitness. Shit.

Our next trip is something I've never heard of until recently, but I can highly recommend. A babymoon - what a brilliant idea. I'm sure the concept has been around for a while, but even still, fantastic! A last break before the wee one arrives and holidays become a different story altogether.

A week after we return from Brisbane, Erin and I are off again, up to Byron Bay for a week. We stay in a swish self-contained apartment with its own pool, and it's a five-minute walk from the beach—about 15 minutes in my condition.

Obviously Erin can't drink, so it ends up being the most sober holiday the two of us have ever had. We watch movies and hobble along the beach, we read books, eat out and dine in, and the best part is that we do whatever the hell we feel like. Despite the ankle situation and the lack of alcohol—it's perfect.

I guess the message is that it might be a good idea to cram in a few trips before the wee one arrives and your life changes forever. Because getting on a plane, relaxing weekends away and all that nice stuff, is all about to disappear.

Getting ready

Back in Sydney afterwards, we start getting ready. All of a sudden Erin has a big bump and looks pregnant, and we buy some baby stuff. Cot, pram, storm cover for pram (although I'm sure if there was a storm you wouldn't be taking your baby out) car seat and sleeping head supporter (what!?). We're given some other bits and pieces—walkie-talkies, a bassinet (a tiny little bed), cot sheets and a pram sleeping bag (hmm, maybe).

We visit obstetricians, have another couple of scans, book into a prenatal course called Calm Birth (yes) and go to a group session run by the Royal Prince Alfred Hospital.

Now that, turns out to be an interesting evening to say the very least. Of the four 'groups' in attendance, we are the only 'regular' couple, and I say group because I'm not too sure how else to describe three women having a baby together. There is another 'more conventional' lesbian couple, and an old English guy (early 60s I'd say) with a young Swedish chic (mid 20s). You've got to love Sydney.

First of all, prompted by the 'slightly hippyish' midwife, all of these total strangers begin discussing methods of preparation for childbirth; what you've been doing so far (nothing), what you're planning on taking into the delivery room with you (eh?) and then, one of them mentions... perineal massage. And, more specifically how that can help loosen things up, so it doesn't *rip* during the main event... my ears prick up somewhat. So it doesn't *rip* during the main event... what the fuck?!

This is the first I've heard of anything like that. A disturbing revelation indeed, and then to add insult to injury we all—that's five lesbians, the old guy and the Swede—discuss how to perform this preparatory massage of the perineum! I don't say, a fucking, word. Neither does

Erin, thank God. Now I've had a few bizarre moments in my life, but this is certainly up there. I've never had an evening like it.

Ah Sydney.

Sleep is a bit more difficult for Erin now, she's a little grumpy and short with people, and I'm sure hormones are a contributing factor in addition to the actual lack of sleep. To address the situation we buy a big long pillow that's supposed to help support the body while you're pregnant. It doesn't really work for Erin, but I love it.

We start getting the room ready, and I finally get my ass into gear with the 'Finding Nemo' painting. It's the first time I've painted anything in about 10 years, so it's pretty slow going but enjoyable. I forgot about the kind of meditative 'zone' you get into when you're concentrating on a painting, and it feels good to be finally doing something tangible for the wee one.

All is going swimmingly as far as I'm concerned, but then Erin seems to be overcome with doubt again. From my perspective all of this has come completely out of the blue, but as Erin spoke, I could tell it had been praying on her mind for a while.

She is worried that she won't able to cope with having a baby; that she won't bond with the peanut. What can you say to that? It'll be fine. Don't worry about it, there are two of us in this, we'll work through it? It's just your hormones. It'll be cool, it'll be fine…? Since time began people have been having babies, even idiots have been having (and managing to bring up) babies, so I think we'll be alright…?

I've since found out that it's pretty common for women, this doubt of bonding and possible failure to cope.

There's not that much you can do except comfort, make cups of tea and reassure.

Overall however, things are going well. It is part of the fabric of life now, constantly there in the background and we're both so looking forward to having this new wee person in our lives. My mum and her partner, Jim, come over from Scotland to visit. As always, it's nice to have family around. A wee taste of home that I really need. It's such an unknown, what we're heading into that the security of family is welcome.

To keep them involved in the process we organise a scan during their trip. The regular black and white pictures are compiled into three-dimensional images at this place, and we see the little one looking like a proper person for the first time ever. Jim actually feels pretty queasy. It's a far cry from when he had his children.

"They go from your lap, to your back" is his oft-quoted advice on becoming a father. "It's a life sentence!"

So Brisbane, Byron, a visit from home, and all of a sudden it is time to go back to work. I was out of work for about two-and-a-half months, and it was bliss. I don't think I'd get bored if I didn't have to work again. Some people moan with too much time on their hands. Not me. I can fill the day just fine thanks. I'd be quite happy never to have to go back. However, got mouths to feed now.

How much is it all going to cost? My facts

In reality, this is an impossible figure. I used to joke that it costs every single penny you've got, plus every penny you're ever going to earn, and then some. I think back when I was throwing that comment around, it was because we were paying for a nanny (there'd been continuous illness), and I was a little overwhelmed. So let's just look at 'set-up' costs for now. We'll get into 'ongoing' costs later.

The items listed here are all you need to buy before the little one arrives, in my opinion anyway. The actual costs depend on how premium you want your baby things to be, and whether you have friends or family who can give you some of the gear they're finished with.

Pram—You can spend as much as you like here. A basic pram from K-Mart—$25, $500 for a decent middle-of-the-road model, and $2,500+ for something ridiculous that Madonna or the Kardashians probably have. We bought a three-wheeled off-roader called a Mountain Buggy. Which was great. We were also talked into the sheepskin rug lining, the storm cover and a few other accessories, but we said no to the lift out capsule. However on reflection, it would have been extremely useful.

So, Mountain Buggy: $450; Mountain Buggy capsule: $150; Storm cover: $41; Sheepskin lining: $89; Sun cover $40; Cover storage bag: $15; Bottle holder: $10

Car seat—$50–$500 and more I'm sure. We bought one from the top of the range here—not an area I wanted to exercise frugality in. You're not allowed to take your child home from the hospital without one of these. You can also buy a car seat that has a 'capsule' attachment—where your baby can fall asleep and you just unlock the capsule to lift it out from the seat. Once again we didn't buy one, but we should have.

So, Car seat: $450; Car seat fitter: $40

Cot—Anywhere from $50 to whatever you want. I think ours was about $200, and $50 for the mattress. Looks nice, does the job—has pull up barriers at the side, adjusts when the wee one gets a bit bigger and converts into a bed when they start climbing out—a multi-purpose bargain.

So, wooden cot and mattress: $250; Bedding: $150

Bassinet—A tiny portable bed. We were given a loan of one and I thought it would be a waste of time. I was wrong. Our kid slept in it for 6 months.

So, bassinet: $100

Change mat, or (more expensive) change table—A bit like an orthopedic pillow that you plonk the little one down on to change a nappy. A change table serves the same purpose, but carries a lot of stuff in the drawers or shelves below. We started off with a change matt, as we had a chest of drawers we thought would do the job with a matt on top, but about two weeks into it I went out to buy a change table—and it was a brilliant buy.

So, change matt: $20; change table: $50-$500+

Baby bag—Very useful. A specially designed bag that hangs almost permanently over the back of the pram. Pockets for nappies, nappy bags, wipes, potions and all sorts of bits and pieces. This will most likely be dealt with by your partner. We *are* talking fashion item here, so depending on how much your partner normally spends on a bag, that'll give you an indication. Google whatever Angelina Jolie had, that's probably the one you'll end up with.

So, baby bag: About $400

Baby bath—Handy if you only have a shower in the house, actually, handy even if you have a bath, as it's a good size for the little one.

So, baby bath: $15-$75

Nappies—One box will do to start with, and will last you about two weeks. We experimented with various brands and always ended up going back to Huggies. They are the most expensive brand but if you like a nappy that works (and I can assure you that's exactly what you want) then you fork out a little extra. If you don't mind shite leaking out right left and centre, buy whatever you want and deal with the consequences.

So, Huggies: $33

Wipes—Get three packs of these to begin with, maybe more, you can never have too many. Ensure they don't have alcohol, are free of parabens and generally free of scent. Less chance of them giving your baby nappy rash that way.

So, wipes x 3: $15

Nappy bin—Not essential, but we were given one of these as a loan and it was pretty handy. It's a special bin with a locking lid, and separate 'tied off' bag components for every single nappy that you deposit into it. Quite good if you live in an apartment, and can't be bothered going up and down the stairs to the bins all the time.

So, nappy bin: $129; Replacement bags: $15

Creams and potions—Vaseline and Sudocrem are the basics here. Vaseline for every day baby bum use, and Sudocrem for whenever the poor blighter has nappy rash. In reality, you'll end up with a whole load more of these types of things. I have no idea how much we spent, or continue to spend, but I do remember going to buy some Papaya Fruit cream for the little one's behind—and it cost about $17 a tube!

So, Vaseline: Family size tub—$15; Sudocrem: Family size tub—$22; baby shampoo: $10

Bottles and teats—You'll need four or five of these to begin with, then later you might want to buy more. It's more complicated than you would think. Different teats fit better with different babies mouths, and you've just got to go with what works best. We had Avent, and they worked a treat.

So, bottles and teats: 4 x $8 = $32

Bottle steriliser—Not sure what people did before these came along. I'm sure we survived just fine, but anyway—essential item nowadays. My mother used to have a steriliser that would boil water around the bottles and would take about half an hour to complete its cycle. We had one that you just stick in the microwave. Did the job in a couple of minutes.

So, steriliser: $110

Breast pump—Only needed if your partner is going to breastfeed. She can express milk into bottles that you can use later to give the little one a bottle of the good stuff, providing a well-earned break for your good lady. This is what I used to do the 'dream feed' at 10pm every night, allowing Erin to sleep through that particular feeding session.

So, breast pump: $170

Baby monitor—You can buy all sorts. Top of the range will have pads that you place under the baby's mattress, alerting you if there hasn't been much movement in a while. You can also get monitors that keep an eye on humidity, temperature, you name it. Humidity and 'movement sensors' we thought was a bit much, so we got an Oricom secure 200-2, that had one transmitter and two receivers. The transmitter could also play a wee bit of music (although we never used it) and had little starry lights (I don't think anyone ever noticed). It kept an eye on the temperature, which was handy, and it broadcast squeals at all times of the day. One of the receivers is in our bedroom, the other in the living room. It's been in constant use for years now, and it's still hanging in there.

So, baby monitor: $125

Baby clothes—One of the good things about the baby shower—if your partner has one—is that you're likely to get a lot of this stuff as presents.

Swaddling wraps—Very important. Wrapping your kid in one of these properly will help them go to sleep—the most important thing in the world. At least seven of these is a good idea, as they'll get covered in sick a lot of the time, and you don't want to run out before you've had time to put a washing on.

So, wraps x 7: $105

Onesies (used to be called a babygro in my day)—This is pretty much all they'll wear for the first couple of months. A onesie is like a leotard for babies. You'll go through a power of these, puke and shit all over them. A good ten will do it.

So, onesies x 10: $50

Vests—To go under or over the onesies.

So, vests x 10: $60

Socks—Daily use.

So, socks x 7: $14

Hat—Depends on where you live, but in general they're not very good at regulating their temperature, so a couple of these, depending on how cold it is, will do the trick. They say that if *you* need a T-shirt, they'll need a jumper; if you need a jumper, they should have a jacket on. You get the gist.

So, hats x 2: $20

Little gloves (mittens)—To keep their hands warm, and also to stop them from scratching their own wee faces. Don't know why they do this.

So, gloves: $5

So there you go, total set-up costs are variable of course. However for us, it was $3,291. What else could you do with that? Buy a jet ski? A week in Fiji? Invest it? I've heard it can cost around $200,000 to bring a child up to the age of 18. Hmm. I think it'll cost more than that, but, we'll see.

11

Thirty-Two Weeks, And A Wee Scare

> *"Family life is full of major and minor crises—the ups and downs of health, success and failure of career, marriage, and divorce—and all kinds of characters. It is tied to places and events and histories. With all of these felt details, life etches itself into memory and personality. It's difficult to imagine anything more nourishing to the soul."*
> —Thomas Moore. **Well said that man.**

The days continue to fly along at a frightening pace, and all of a sudden Erin is 32 weeks in. We could have a baby literally any day now.

It is time to go on our Calm Birth course. Again, something I've never heard of before. Why would I? In short, Calm Birth is about trying to give birth without the use of drugs. It's a bit hippyish, and being a bit of a hippy deep down, I'm quite looking forward to hearing all about it. We're just about to head out the door when Erin mentions there's a little bit of blood. Not much, just a wee bit she says, not sure if it's anything to worry about, really…

"Are you sure about that? Has this happened before? Should we not go to the hospital just to double check?"

"No, it's just a tiny bit, I'm sure it's fine…"

So, while Erin heads up to the street, and I head down to the basement to bring the car up, this quick little conversation begins to sink in. By the time Erin gets in the car at the top, we've both decided that it's probably best to head to the hospital, just to be sure. It's nothing really, but let's just drop into the hospital on the way to the Calm Birth course.

It's nothing really.

Meanwhile, an uneasy feeling starts to rise in my stomach and at the back of my throat. Then a voice inside my head says 'Who are you trying to kid? You're driving your pregnant wife to the hospital, she's 32 weeks in, and she's bleeding!'

And it doesn't stop there. This is why the human mind is a dangerous instrument. This other fucking person who's taken control of my thoughts decides to introduce a scenario that appears to have only one purpose. To terrify the life out of me.

Erin's phone is on its last legs and can only send text messages. We'd planned to buy a new one soon, and as we're driving to hospital I suddenly think it's important for her to have a working phone before we get there.

Like, why on earth would she need a mobile phone? Where the hell am I going to be, apart from right next to her?

Anyway, I think, for a fraction of a second, that we should swing by an electronics store and pick up a cheap mobile phone… on the way to the hospital, with my wife who's pregnant, 32 weeks in, and bleeding.

And within that fraction of a second's thought, a scenario plays out in my mind where dreadful things happen, and we're minutes too late to the hospital to do anything about it, because of a stupid trip to by a $20 phone.

What the fuck?! Why do I do this kind of shit to myself?

We head straight to the hospital. Me, Erin, the 'nut, and her busted old phone are taken through to the prenatal clinic and admitted into an examination room.

The nurse is very kind and patient. She gets Erin lying down, attaches a couple of pads to the bump so we can hear the baby's heartbeat, and the machine next to the bed starts running a printout. We're told to wait until one of the doctors is free, and in the meantime the monitor records what we all hope will be a regular rhythm. She brings through some magazines, and we're back in hospital time —ahh. Oh look! There's a *New Idea*.

The nurse comes through after half-an-hour to tell us the doctor is in surgery and might be a while. Surgery. A word I don't want to hear. Bleeding, pregnancy and hospitals. Not a great combination. I nip out to call the Calm Birth lady, and the doctor arrives just as I return.

Much like the lovely nurse, I like him instantly. And it dawns on me how important that is. Because it means that I trust him. Just from his calm and friendly demeanor, I am more at ease about what is going on, even though we still don't know what is going on.

The baby's heartbeat is fine, so that's good. The blood is discussed, the fact that there's no accompanying pain, and the fact that there is no glaringly obvious reason for the bleeding—all of these are positive signs.

But the main worry with bleeding is that it might mean trouble with the placenta. If that's been ruptured, it's big trouble in little China. We already know that Erin's placenta is a little low, so they schedule another scan for the following day.

And when there's bleeding involved, it's standard practice to keep a pregnant woman in for 24 hours. Oh. Hospital for the night, then. Not expecting that.

Although we're using the public health system for the birth, we can use our private health insurance for a room in the hospital and, thankfully, one is available.

The nurse comes back with a wheelchair that she insists Erin gets into, before ushering her through to the postnatal ward and her room for the night. Erin's protestations fall on deaf ears and it is almost funny, before I realise how close we are to needing that wheelchair for real. A sobering thought. One that helps me bite my tongue and just be happy with the situation; appreciating that we're not in more dire circumstances like the hundreds of people around us.

A night in hospital

It's a standard hospital room, but at least it's a room for one. It even has an en-suite and a tiny TV bracketed to the wall at the foot of the bed. We call a number scribbled on a little notice board beside the phone for it to work.

Hospital television rental. $8 for 24 hours. $7.90 if you have private health insurance. Credit card details up front. TV will come on in about 20 minutes.

Talk about the unexpected costs of becoming a parent! There was nothing in the spreadsheet for this. Thankfully the private health insurance saves us more than 10 cents on the TV however. The room, on its own, is just under $500 for the night. Think about that when you're deciding if you need private health insurance or not.

Erin finishes a long and detailed list of the things she needs from home, including the location of said items, for her overnight stay in the RPA Hilton. Just as I'm about to go however, the telly comes on. We flick around and find a movie just starting on the Hallmark channel, so we lie together on Erin's single hospital bed, with the sound coming out of the remote control (which also has the panic button on it, that we accidentally push a couple of times) and it's very relaxing.

We manage to chill and watch some mindless drivel for a while, fazing out what's actually going on. Nice. Required. Decompression time.

After my visit home to pack up all the bits and pieces (I forget the towel) I head back to the hospital. Niamh arrives and we talk some bullshit to distract from the fact we are all sitting in hospital, and then we watch some bullshit too—'Masterchef'.

I leave to go home and realise it is the first night we've been apart in years. It's a little unsettling leaving Erin there. Fairly sure all will be well of course, but still, somewhat strange. The next day I get a call at work saying there is more bleeding and I rush back to the hospital. We get the all clear again, Erin goes home and I speed back to work just in time for a meeting.

All in all a pretty hectic little episode, a real scare and a reminder that we're not quite home and dry yet.

Health insurance: The facts
If you'd like to have private health insurance for the main event, or your pediatrician, you should know that many of the providers (in Australia) won't cover you unless you upgrade your plan to 'family' at least a couple of months before falling pregnant.

If you upgrade today and do the job tonight, you might not be covered. Kids are going to cost enough as it is, make sure you get this right. Three months was what our health fund required, funnily enough the same length of time it takes for your body to produce sperm from scratch... just saying.

12

Calm Birth, Calm Life

"I think I was in Amsterdam at the time."
— Unnamed Scottish father. **Calm birth, old school style.**

We finally make it along to Calm Birth a couple of weeks later, and I must admit it turns out to be a lot more enjoyable than I was expecting.

As I said, and as the name suggests, it's about staying calm whilst giving birth. The course teaches relaxation techniques that lessen the pain during childbirth so the mother doesn't need any drugs. A feat that is easier said than done I would imagine, but not impossible, as I probably once would have thought. Had I ever given any thought to child birth at all before now. It's just not something that a bloke thinks about, well I certainly hadn't. Even up until the point of going to the course.

At this point I'd only just found out I was expected to be in the room. I guess I kind of thought I'd be pacing around outside, going for endless cups of crappy coffee and waiting for some doctor to bring me the news: "It's a boy Mr McLeod." Have you seen 'Mad Men'? Like that, but with less whisky.

My dad sat in the waiting room while I was delivered, and he was under strict instructions from the doctor to watch and later relay all that happened in the final episode of Colditz. My timing proving a little inconvenient for the good doctor who'd religiously followed one of the most popular drama series of the 1970s, only to have it all ruined by my arrival.

A Scottish friend of mine approaching parenthood asked his father where *he* was during the birth, and the reply was, "I think I was in Amsterdam at the time."

Or maybe, I suppose if I had thought about it, maybe I'd be in the room for a little while towards the end, holding Erin's hand as she screams and shouts and tells me to shut the fuck up. "Push honey, push, harder, yeah that's it." Hollywood, and the 70s have a lot to answer for. All that Le Mas course and quick breathing crap? Apparently quick breathing is about the worst thing you can do.

The lowdown—The uterus, where the baby lives before birth, has two sets of muscles. One set that contracts, and pushes the baby down and out, and another set that holds the cervix (the exit) closed.

The first set of muscles does its business automatically—the contractions. It's all set off by a hormone that's issued by the baby, letting mum know, "Time's up, I'm ready to come out now". So the woman's body just heads off doing what it's been programmed to do. Easy.

The problems begin with the second set of muscles, which seem determined to keep the emergency exit shut. This doesn't stop or deter the contractions from trying to push the baby out, and the result is extreme pain. Even more than the woman is experiencing already.

The crux of the whole deal, is trying to get yourself to relax, to allow the muscles around the cervix just to open up as they should, rather than tensing them up. I've heard the comparison before, like trying to shit a rugby ball… now, imagine trying to relax while that's going on.

The course goes through some theory, scientific reasoning, and all sorts of interesting stuff, but at the end of the day you have to learn to stay calm, when all hell is breaking loose.

We go through lots of relaxation techniques and practice them on and off throughout the day, which is great for someone with a bit of a hangover—I almost doze off a couple of times. Deep and steady breathing, visualisation techniques, all very useful for life in general, never mind getting through this monumental event of childbirth.

That's another thing I learn from the course, the gravity of it. Also, the fact it doesn't have to be a chore. Believe it or not there are women out there who have a fantastic time during childbirth; they actually enjoy the experience! Who would have thought that!

My perspective afterwards however, is completely different. It sounds like an amazing event. Not just something dreadful that you have to endure to bring a wee person into the world, but a joyous and wonderful occasion in its own right. I almost can't wait!

I know I'm not the one about to go through it and all, but the feelings of overwhelming emotion and love that permeate the new family immediately after the birth? All that sounds freakin' awesome, bring it on!

Overall the supposedly 'dreaded' prenatal classes turn out to be quite interesting. And, once again if I was to offer any advice here, I'd say keep an open mind, don't go with a hangover, and don't dread it so much. You might even enjoy yourself.

Life in general was pretty emotional back then. But despite the ups and the downs, in between all of it I was much more content than usual. Things were going well and I often found myself just happy to be alive. It was all building to the birth of this new wee person of course, and the change they were about to have in our lives.

I felt even closer to Erin, and I found myself loving her even more than before. A wonderful feeling of contentment... Jesus, talk about emotional wreck. And that's even before the freaking birth!

The final countdown

Although Erin isn't terribly bothered about having a baby shower, her friends are all up for it. Back in Scotland and Ireland it's not really done. Not by anyone that we ever knew anyway—but it seems to be the way to go in Australia.

After being talked into doing it, Erin has a lovely day. She gets to see friends she hasn't seen for ages and, although we stocked up on the champagne, there was hardly a person drinking. Half of them were pregnant or had kids to look after—I guess we're just reaching that age.

The other good thing about a baby shower, is that it gives me an excuse to clear out and catch up with a few pals. We arrange to go to a wee nine-hole golf course at Bondi and thankfully it's a beautiful day. It's a good mixture of people, and a good laugh, certainly not serious golf. Beers in the clubhouse, and then onto some pub afterwards.

Home early, around 10–10:30pm and that's it. A lot of the chat is about the impending parental situation, pram pros and cons... stirring stuff.

Once you've passed all the scans and that 32-week milestone, you enter what I've heard referred to as 'the drop zone'. Very appropriate. You're just waiting. Waiting for it all to happen. And it's a weird little period in life.

Looking back on it now, shit...I'm glad we had a nice relaxed last couple of weeks.

Although it's been reasonably plain sailing between the two of us there's still the odd moment of contention, hormones playing up with Erin. I got a going over once, not because I didn't make the bed, but because I didn't make it properly! All very minor in the grand scheme of things. And Erin did call me up later that day to say sorry.

She is also very uncomfortable, tired a lot and finding it extremely difficult to sleep. I soon discover that if Erin's not sleeping well—then I'm not sleeping well, and one night in particular I can't sleep at all. Nothing to do with Erin. I wonder if it's my body preparing itself for the onslaught that life is about to throw at me? Who knows, anyway, I get up and Skype Fraser in Costa Rica, catch up on the last seven months or so. Turns out they're pregnant again, only a couple of months behind us.

I also take advantage of this last little period of time to get on with the Finding Nemo mural I've promised to myself and the little one. Mural as it turns out is a bit beyond the time available, but I am pleased with the cheery little starfish I paint. The rest of Nemo's gang, on a larger canvas, is still unfinished in the garage, I'd say will probably remain there for at least another couple of years.

But hey, life is filled with good intentions... at least the little starfish makes it into being.

13

Life Interrupted

"The illusion of control – the number one human addiction."
—Iyanla Van Zant. **And a hard one to break.**

Four weeks 'till D-day, just after a game of golf and one of the guys says, "Oh I imagine we'll sneak another game in before the baby's due eh?"

That's when it hits home. Actually no, could be some time before I'm heading out for another game. It could be a while before I'm doing lots of things again. I was keen to have one last big blow out with my mates, and suddenly it's too late. Can't be too drunk when any minute there could be a desperate rush to the hospital. A few beers, sure, but not the last blast I was hoping for.

Nine months has flown by. My outlook and perspective has changed radically, but even still I can hardly believe the baby is virtually knocking on the door. I really feel as if I am ready for this next 'stage' in life though, and we're both very much looking forward to it.

Lots of other things seem to be falling into place too. My new job is working out well, and I'm doing some freelance copywriting which is bringing in a bit of extra cash.

I even come home from work with a smile on my face more often than not. I'm making a real difference to the business and people are noticing, which is nice for a change. I was given the employee of the month award, in my first month! Amazing! All I was doing was my job, I was quite embarrassed.

It is very satisfying that people think I deserved it, but I didn't quite know what to say except, a simple thanks. Nobody's ever said well done in a job prior to this, now they're giving me a trophy and putting my name on the wall! Only took me 16 years to find a workplace that's not full of assholes.

Then, just as I'm beginning to think it's all under control, Erin calls and says, "I think you'd better sit down". An opening like that—I leave the office. She explains that our already very small baby, has stopped growing— indicating a possible issue with the placenta, which is the life support system.

The result is that the peanut is now at the, 'we're worried' size, and they're going to whip the kid out pronto. That's not quite how she puts it, but that's the gist. "They're going to take me in and induce me on Monday".

It is a bit of a shock to say the least. From a month up our sleeve to a couple of days. Just like that. Life, interrupted. Erin seems alright about it though; not too worried or upset. She has a few chores to do, heading out to get the baby seat fitted in the car—good timing—then into town, then home. I'm ready to leave straight away but she seems fairly together, so I decide to finish up a bit early instead. Saving my time off for when the wee one has arrived.

After the fact, asking Erin about this, and how she felt about being told she had days as opposed to weeks before the little one was due, she told me she wasn't quite as together as she had appeared. Her main emotions were shock, and disbelief, followed by stress and worry. Shock because the decision seemed to have come out of nowhere, and worry, because if they wanted the peanut out that quickly, then surely there must have been something wrong.

I try to leave at 4pm, but get caught up doing some shitty excel spreadsheet that I just can't get to work. It drives me up the wall, and the more I struggle the stronger I feel the urge to head home.

Eventually I just give up, frustrated, and almost run out of the office. Straight down to the train station, straight down to the wrong platform, and straight onto the wrong train. I have this faint sense that something isn't quite right, so I ask a passenger where the train is heading…Fuck! I *just* manage to stop the door from closing, and force it open while a conductor shouts at me.

"Fuck off!" I shout back as I run up the stairs, and over to the other side like a wild man. 'I'm going to have a fucking baby!'

Seated on the correct train and heading in the right direction, the Glaswegian in me recedes and I begin to relax. I even manage a pleasant walk home. Put some good music on (The Joshua Tree) and enjoy the evening, the fresh air and the feeling of excitement and energy that's flowing through me. I stop, buy some flowers and a couple of lottery tickets. 'I'm going to have a baby!'

The minute I walk in the front door the phone rings, Erin is in the kitchen and I don't even get to say hi before she is talking to her brother John. After a couple of minutes I have to go through and ask her to hang up. We hug and she starts to cry. We switch all the phones off, talk, and come to terms with it. She is worried that there's something wrong with the wee fella. "It's a small baby and isn't growing anymore" she says. So what, I counter, we're only small people ourselves, and it's been long enough for the little one to come out.

Anyway, hormones playing up, and the outside possibility that there actually *might* be something wrong… who knows…I can't let my mind explore that possibility though. It's Tuesday, so I only have to get through the next couple of days at work, then I take the Friday off.

That's the week I also make it onto TV. A news crew shoves a camera in my face as I turn away from a ticket machine at the train station. I had just discovered that the trains were free that day, and they ask me what I think of it. "Well it's better than having to bloody pay for them isn't it!" mumbles this blustering Scotsman with a wry smile on his face. How stereotypical, they probably packed up after they got the footage. Gruff Scotsman enjoys not paying for the train. Job done.

Anyway, my TV debut aside, Friday we head in for another scan. We're booked into the hospital on Sunday night, to be induced on Monday, but if things don't look too hot on Friday at the scan, they'll just keep us in and go for it. We pack all our bags and leave the house at 2:30 pm, prepared to have a baby.

We don't have the baby that day as it turns out, and we return home fairly knackered a couple of hours later.

We wake up the next morning knowing these are our last few moments before it all kicks off, so we go to nice restaurants, eat our favourite foods, watch TV and walk along Sydney harbour foreshore. Very relaxing, very nice, very calm.

The main event: What to take

Our preparations were informed by the RPA prenatal course and the Calm Birth course. Both a little hippyish, but both helped us approach child birth feeling as if we had done at least something to get ready, as opposed to just turning up and hoping for the best.

We were given a CD to listen to at the Calm Birth course, which we were supposed to listen to every night. We managed every three or four nights, and it helped with breathing and visualisation techniques. I liked it, Erin not so much—but it formed part of our preparations and, Erin says now, it helped her when it counted.

We also took relaxing music on an iPod, and a wee speaker system (I can never listen to 'The Mission' soundtrack ever again) and I think this must have been Calm Birth influenced too.

On a more practical level we took a load of food; frozen casserole, muesli bars, power bars and Lucozade. Although we weren't expecting 'one of those births' that go on forever we were certainly prepared for one, and we had been told that maintaining your energy levels becomes extremely important if you end up being in there for days.

The main event: The birth plan

This is where you decide in advance, what your response is going to be to a number of key questions. It means you can decide in a sensible, considered manner in your living room weeks before hand—as opposed to right in the middle of the most stressful situation you've ever experienced. That way you don't even have to think about it, the answers are there already—discussed and agreed upon. For example, drugs? And if so, what type, and how many? And, once the new one arrives there are a number of injections that most hospitals like to deliver straight away. Are you happy with that? Or would you rather wait a wee while before sticking your newborn with a needle.

I wrote this in my diary just before we head off to hospital.

'Sunday 15 August 2010—1:54pm. Going in to have a baby in three hours from now. This time last week we thought we had a month left.'

'Sunday 15 August 2010—4:34pm. Leaving in ten minutes to go to the hospital. Everything's packed and ready, bags waiting at the door like we're about to go on holiday. What we think life is going to be like:

Erin: Initially—great relief that it's all gone well. Then a couple of weeks of noisy chaos—then we'll be fine. Going to be exciting, and great to have our own little family, the three of us as opposed to the two of us.

Me: I think it's going to be great, we have to go now!'

So here we are, heading off on Sunday 15 August to have a baby. At least we have a plan.

14

Here We Go …

"Everybody has a plan, until they get punched in the face."
—Mike Tyson. **Tru dat.**

We arrive at the Royal Prince Alfred Hospital and we're shown to one of those $500 a night rooms. It's a decent size, thank goodness, and it even has a pullout bed for me. Happy days. $7.90 for the TV and we're set.

A nurse appears and interrupts our viewing to explain the induction process.

First, they introduce hormones into the cervix, and with a bit of luck this kick starts the birth. You go to sleep for the night, let the hormones do their job, and within 12 hours the body is supposed to take over and do its thing. So we're hoping for it to start tomorrow morning. The hormones can sometimes bring the first stages of labour on within a couple of hours, but we're not really expecting that to happen as Erin is still three weeks away from the due date.

If this initial step doesn't work then a hormone gel is applied. You wait for six hours. Then another round of gel, another six hours and if nothing's happening by then, they hook you up to a cyntosin drip—which is a kick in the ass and really pushes things along.

The cyntosin is pretty overwhelming. It takes you from nothing, to full on—without the normal, gradual build-up that would help you get used to the severity of the heavier contractions. It's an intense experience, which is why it's left as a last resort.

We both hope it doesn't get to that. The initial induction stages try and gently nudge the body into labour, and let it do its own thing from there on. Sounds good, let's have some of that then.

Once we're settled in a doctor appears, and after an 'all too brief' introduction, he performs a cervix examination. Fuck. Here we go. Now even though it doesn't sound like a particularly nice procedure to begin with; take my word for it, it's even worse in reality. I see the concentration on Erin's face as she breathes her way through this very first step—thanks Calm Birth.

Only one centimetre dilated. We need 10 centimetres for birth, so they insert the hormones and off we go. I focus on Erin's face, trying to send her strength. Brave girl, she breathes her way through it yet again, but I can tell it is a powerfully uncomfortable sensation. In fact I'm sure uncomfortable doesn't quite cut it as a descriptor. I really can't imagine, or don't want to.

I feel helpless and fiercely protective. Tensed up. A tight ball of muscle, definitely in 'fight' as opposed to 'flight' mode. I could take Mike Tyson if he got in my way right now. I guess it's situations like these that our instincts have evolved to deal with.

So we're aiming for 12 hours. Go to sleep, wake up, go into labour, have a baby by dinner time, bite to eat, then we can all get a good night's sleep. I'm serious, that's the plan, discussed and agreed upon. It looks promising. Erin thinks she can feel some cramps a bit like period pain, but isn't too sure... let's stick to the plan.

Sophie and her husband James come to visit. Then James and I wander into Newtown for takeaway dinner. Very civilised. Hardly what you would imagine a birth to be like. They leave and we watch a new TV drama about a girl who works in a maternity ward. Jees.

Once again however, the peanut doesn't care what our plan is, and 12 hours come and go without movement. We wake up Sunday morning to nothing but disgusting hospital food, and a nurse telling us we'd be better off eating McDonalds from round the corner.

Anyway, another examination and we're still only one centimetre. On goes the gel. The cramps come on much quicker this time, and when Erin is kneeling on the bed moaning but saying she's fine, I text Sophie.

"It's staring, albeit slowly."

Sophie is Erin's second birth partner, with me the first of course. She's been a birth partner before, so having been there and done that, and being the person that she is, we both couldn't imagine anybody better to have by our side.

And having Sophie there turns out to be one of the best decisions we could have hoped for.

Erin climbs down off the bed and finds it much more comfortable walking around. The midwife says if we want to go for a walk then feel free, so off we go.

We intend to walk around the grass just outside the hospital, but end up wandering the back streets of Newtown and Camperdown for a good couple of hours.

Sophie joins us during our walkabout. We stop in for coffee, sausage rolls, and even drop into a candle shop for a look around. It's weird. Here we are mid-labour, strolling around looking at candles. You would never think when you see a pregnant woman walking down King Street that she's actually in labour. Well, actually, maybe, on King St…

Anyway, we get back to the hospital, back to the room and hunker down.

Erin's initial discomfort has mostly passed, only coming back now and again. The midwife, Sister Ignatius, comes in to see how she is doing and comments "You don't look like a woman in labour".

And she's right. Erin is lying on the bed reading a magazine and we were all having a laugh about something or other. I certainly don't feel like my wife is in the middle of giving birth. Before too long however, there is absolutely no mistaking the fact that we ain't in Kansas anymore Toto.

The doctor returns around 2pm and we're all hoping for further dilation. If not, our schedule is now pushed out to at least 8pm. Not ideal, but manageable. We might still get a decent nights sleep. Once they decide the second stage of labour has begun they are going to move us down into the delivery ward, and that's where it all begins in earnest.

The doctor reports no further dilation but continued softening of the cervix—which is something at least. No move to the delivery ward however. More gel and another six hour wait instead. The cramps come on quickly as before, but much stronger this time, and it's not long until Erin is pacing up and down the room, hands on the small of her back, belly pushed out and beginning to zone the two of us out. OK, now we're talking. Throughout all of this, Sophie always seems to know exactly what to do, and when the pacing has done all that it can, she suggests Erin gets in the shower. And sitting in that wee seat in the shower, is where she stays for the next 2—3 hours.

We check in on her now and again. Erin and I have a hand signal so she can let me know she's still OK, despite the fact that she looks far from it and isn't that interested in communicating with the outside world at all. I'm glad we have it though, it works pretty well when I can see her in such discomfort without being able to help.

Sophie and I have a couple of games of cards, then watch some episodes of MASH. Surreal. 8pm finally rolls around and we are convinced that we'll be heading downstairs to the delivery room. Not much more dilation this time either, but sufficient progress for us all to head down anyway. At last. We've already packed up in preparation. Sophie takes a wee trolley with our gear, and I walk beside Erin holding her arm. Into the breach we go…

Delivery room 5. It's huge but comfortable, and the ensuite has a bath and a shower, which Erin is over the moon about. The shower upstairs had really been helping so she was looking forward to the water. I have my swimming trunks packed, ready to go.

Another midwife arrives and I take an instant dislike to her. We all do. Erin is lying on the bed and I'm holding her hand. This woman comes over and says that I'm going to be in the way. "Move" she says. I could have hit her. I refrain, and oblige for now by sitting on a chair a couple of metres away. She proceeds to put a cannula in Erin's arm that she'll need later when, and if, they start the cyntosin drip. Meanwhile I sit there dying to harm this woman. Staring at her so intently I'm half expecting her to spontaneously combust right here in the delivery room.

She doesn't go into much detail on what our options are from here, just finalises the cannula and attaches a monitor to the bump. This is because the peanut we're expecting is a small one and we'll need the monitor to check on the heartbeat. The midwife upstairs had told us that if you get the monitor with the wires, then you can't jump in and out of the water—so ask for the wireless one and you'll be fine. The woman who is with us now doesn't even mention it, and only when we specifically ask does she say, "Oh yeah, I'll go and get one of those monitors if you want". I do not like this woman. Not one little bit. When the doctor arrives he lays it all out for us.

The cyntosin drip, as we know, will really get it moving, but we can wait for an hour to see if Erin dilates any further on her own. We decide to wait, and with our remote monitor pads firmly attached, it's into the shower. The bath is out of the question, even for the remote monitor, but the shower does the trick. Time seems to warp in a delivery ward, so god knows how long we're in there before a new face appears at the door and breaks into a big smile "Hi my name's Natalie, and I'm going to be your midwife for the evening." I instantly feel like a weight has been lifted. She just radiates warmth. "If you need anything just let me know, I'll be back in a while, as you all seem to be doing just fine for now."

What she's talking about is Erin in the buff on her knees, Sophie and me either side with shower heads rinsing her down like a freakin' dolphin. Imagine going to work every day and seeing that!

Eventually we have to go back into the room, and Erin gets onto the bed just as the doctor returns. Not much progress, so it is time to break the waters.

Now, a couple of days ago, Erin told me she'd heard this procedure is excruciatingly painful, and if it comes to it she'd like to take pain relief before hand. Our plans of Calm Birth had been thrown out of the window by now anyway. That had been for a regular, straight down the line normal birth, which this most certainly was not. So if there are drugs, bring 'em on. Unfortunately, we're informed that you can't take anything for this particular step. Then he attaches a little hook to the end of his finger, and goes to work.

It's horrible, but Erin is stoic. After it's done however she is in real trouble. Zoning out and losing control. I'm standing right beside her, *with* her as much as I can be, but she's off, on her own, losing it. I remember the course, how the Calm Birth woman described someone losing their concentration in the pain, and their mind would enter a downward spiral. This is exactly what's happening now. I almost shout, come on Erin, stay with me, breathe, take deep breaths, concentrate.

It all sounds so paltry in the face of such obvious agony and distress. But she pulls it together yet again, and I am utterly amazed at the way she manages it. Pretty sure I'd have lost the plot completely.

This is one of the worst moments of the whole birth. Watching Erin in such agony, unable to do anything about it is the most difficult thing of all.

Sophie is constantly making suggestions throughout, helping Erin breathe, arranging cushions, suggesting I sit with her between my legs, heating up hot packs (which really help) and generally just saying the right thing at the right time. I'm doing all that I can, but Sophie just seems to instinctively know what to do.

No rest for the wicked however. Not long after Erin pulls herself together, the cyntosin drip goes in. We'd talked about pain relief options with Natalie, and gas just wasn't going to cut it, so it was either morphine or epidural. Although it's completely Erin's decision, we discuss it, and Erin wants my opinion.

She is already feeling a bit woozy. A reaction from another injection she had taken to prevent her from throwing up in response to the cyntosin. And while morphine might help with the pain, it will most likely make her feel even more queasy.

We decide to hang in there for as long as possible, skip the morphine and go straight to the epidural when the time comes. Which isn't long. As the cyntosin dose and the intensity of the contractions increases, the pain starts getting the better of her again. If things progress as normal we're still about eight hours away from an actual birth. That's too long. Erin can hold out for a while—but not eight hours, and it's not going to be getting any easier. Onto the epidural, which is where they inject painkiller directly into your spine. It's a fairly specialised task, as you can imagine, and our anaesthetist is brilliant.

He is a calm, collected and patient American gent, and he just fills us with confidence. He explains to Erin exactly what is about to happen, what she will feel and what it will do. He pauses, as Erin goes through more contractions, and when we're all ready he sets up an automatic, slow injection system into her spine. It takes half an hour during which time Erin feels a numbness slowly come over her legs. Once it's finished, the epidural is complete.

So, now that's out of the way, Natalie advises us all to get a bit of sleep. What?!

I can hardly believe that in the middle of all that is going on we get our heads down for a wee kip. Sophie sleeps on the sofa bed, and I'm on the floor right next to Erin. Unbelievable.

I wake up about two hours later, with Natalie beside Erin and cries of 'push!'. Bloody hell, we're on! I clamber up. Now before we'd put our heads down, Natalie said that Erin would still take another six hours or so to fully dilate, but here we are. Here we fucking are!

The epidural has been switched off, so that Erin can feel what's going on in order to push in the right places. Natalie says that as she pushes the pain is temporarily relieved. We'll see. I can certainly tell the pain is returning, and the contractions are huge. The level of the cyntosin drip is up to 210, having started down at 80.

We've now entered into that bit you see on TV where the woman is bearing down with all her might, squeezing her husband's hand and screaming. There's usually a few expletives thrown in, and it looks like something from The Exorcist. According to what we'd been told this is also the 'most painful' part, and should only take an hour or so...

Three hours later a doctor called Joyce says she's going to have to help if that's OK with us. Too fucking right that's OK Joyce. Let's get on with it. Natalie and Sophie have been able to see the head for a couple of hours, but the wee fella just doesn't want to take that last leap into the world, and Erin's body isn't quite ready to give it up, so yes, please, help. Erin is so knackered and in such agony that we'll do anything to get the feckin' peanut out now.

Joyce explains that she can use a suction cup first off, and if that doesn't work then she'll use forceps. She lays out the pros and cons of both, and the possible long—term effects. Nothing that bad at all really, fire away, do whatever you can. Get the fucker out.

I stay up at Erin's head during all of this. I don't really want to have a look down below. Earlier, Natalie and Sophie had been checking out the baby's head, with a torch... No interest in that thank you very much.

So the cup is literally a little cap, about the size of a jam jar lid, attached to the baby's head. It also has a length of string hanging out of it, with a handle on the other end like a starter on a two stroke outboard. Erin manages three more almighty pushes, and she's done in, that's it, there's no way she can manage any more. Joyce talks her into another three. She is a little woman. We'd met her before over the previous couple of weeks and she was quite lovely, but I tell you there's no freakin' messing with her now.

She is controlled, but very firm. "Now Erin, we need three more big pushes, and that's it, that's all we need, come on now Erin. That's it, harder, more, keep going, that's good, now harder."

She doesn't let up, and man, she strains on that fucking handle, it's unreal, it looks as if she could do with lifting her foot up on the edge of the bed to get better leverage, then suddenly, here it is... a tiny wee head pops out.

And on the next push, a whole freakin' person slithers out, and is placed on Erin's chest. Fuck, me! After a couple of seconds, the baby produces an almighty scream and everybody in the room cheers, except for us. Erin breaks into a pained grimace, and I start crying... we've done it.

It's not all over yet though. The placenta that's faithfully fed and nourished the little one for its entire journey so far is now useless and has to be jettisoned.

The placenta can be birthed naturally, or you can get it out a bit quicker with the help of a further injection. Virtually no hesitation in that decision, let's get it over and done with. Even with the injection however, it takes another 10 minutes or so, during which time I notice there are loads of people in the room.

I'm not sure if they've been there all along, or if they've just arrived. Regardless, they are all gowned up in either white, green or blue, signifying their different roles I presume, whatever those are. There is also a lot of blood. And a bucket to collect it in. Joyce keeps asking for more sponges, and calling in more doctors and support. The chief Consultant comes in eventually, then his mobile phone goes off and he actually fucking answers it! He says that he's in theatre and will have to call back, nice as you like. So I'm beginning to realise that what's going on isn't exactly normal.

I'm still up at Erin's head and we're holding the baby—which is a girl by the way—when Joyce asks me to move over and out of the way. Sophie comes with me, and I take

Katie, holding her close to my chest. I've taken my top off so she gets skin to skin and warmth for her first hours in the world... more Calm Birth hippy stuff.

I'm sitting over on Erin's right, about three metres away, looking at her and concentrating on her face. I can't help myself from looking down, there's at least five doctors all covered in blood and a bright red stain on the bottom of Erin's bed. The Consultant says to Erin, "We're going to have to take you into theatre now, you're losing a lot of blood and we have to stop it. We're not sure exactly what it is, but we have to go now."

Sophie puts a blanket round my shoulders, keeping us warm as I sit there watching Erin get rolled out of delivery room 5, blood pouring from the bed as they go. All of a sudden, where moments before there must've been about 10 people all fussing around, there's just me, Katie and Sophie.

As I look at the empty room, and I wish I'd told Erin that I love her, it is, literally, the worst moment of my life. Following on so quickly on from the best. Extreme joy, to shock, to fear, mixed in with sleep deprivation and the mental stress of it all. I'm a total mess, but Sophie holds me together.

The midwife we liked, Natalie, had finished her 12-hour shift meanwhile, and we're back to ol' sour face. Fuck off is my first thought. She says to take lots of pictures so Erin won't miss out on these first few moments of Katie's life, and after half an hour, she takes Katie to weigh her, measure her length and check her responses—she is perfect... of course.

After an hour of clock watching, the consultant comes back in and I hold my breath. She is fine, he says, they had given her a general anaesthetic, taken her through to theatre and she had just stopped bleeding. They had examined and found no remains of the placenta, no tearing, nothing.

Because Erin's labour had gone on for so long her uterus was literally exhausted, and after the effort involved in getting Katie out, it didn't have the energy to contract back down to size again. This left a whole load of exposed blood vessels that just spewed blood. From the time of the bleeding, to when they got her into theatre—about 20 minutes—the uterus had had its rest and contracted back again, closing off the bleeding.

Erin lost 2.6 litres of blood and was on the verge of having to receive a transfusion, but she was OK. Thank god. She was still under the effects of the anaesthetic but would come out of it soon. We're all to catch up back where we started, in the neonatal ward.

I can hardly hold myself together, I'm so thankful. Sophie fusses around, packing bags, and I can hardly move. She feeds me cups of tea, chocolate bars, sandwiches. Eventually the midwife tells us it's time to go, Erin is back upstairs and we're to join her there. Bullshit, we have to wait another 45 minutes, at the end of which of course I'm beginning to fret again.

You can imagine the tears when Erin eventually arrives in a wheelchair. 'I love you so much', we hug, and I put Katie in her arms. Breathe…

So that was it. Childbirth. Not so Calm, Birth. Fuck. Me. What an unbelievable trip. It was so much more than I imagined it would be. More intense, more difficult, more everything, just incredible. One of life's amazing experiences. Unfucking real.

You try to prepare in your mind for the actual event, like training for a marathon. We'd done the courses, we'd practiced the breathing exercises, staying calm, visualisations, we'd even made a plan... but nothing could have prepared us for the reality of it all.

We were admitted into hospital on Sunday 15 August. The proceedings began around 7pm and it wasn't until 8:44am on Tuesday morning that little Katie graced us with her presence. She wasn't even that little. She was 2.7 kilograms, not the 2.1 they predicted from the ultrasounds, bringing her over the 2.5 'you're a small baby and we're worried about you' level.

It was three weeks before the due date, but Katie didn't know about that. Time was irrelevant, and whatever control we thought we had over our lives was about to disappear—or maybe it was never there in the first place—but let's not get overly existential about it.

Welcome to the world little Katie... I love you.

15

Life Begins

"There are three stages of a man's life: He believes in Santa Claus, he doesn't believe in Santa Claus, he is Santa Claus."
—Unknown. **I'll claim that one then.**

The first day is brilliant. Although it's a bit of a daze, everything feels right, life as it's meant to be. I'm so happy with Erin, Katie, me, just everything really.

I receive lots of texts from people saying congratulations, but the one that captures it best, is from my friend Jules.

Apart from the usual congratulations, he says to make sure I savour these precious first few days—they pass quickly and you'll never get them back, so don't be in a rush to get back into the real world again. And that's it, he's right. This bubble of happiness and contentment is so perfect. I don't ever want it to go away. Erin and Katie are less than a couple of metres from me, and that's exactly how I'd like to keep it.

In fact, I find often when there's a quiet moment, tears just spring into my eyes. I sit in our hospital room for hours, just looking at Katie sleeping there in her wee perspex cot, amazed at how beautiful she is. Emotional wreck, as expected.

I wander down the street to get some fresh air and the buzz goes with me. From 'not that keen' about having a kid to this? What a turnaround. I feel as if I've just joined the human race having been sitting on the sideline all these years.

We spend another week in hospital. Erin recovers quickly and doesn't need a transfusion, while Katie has several issues, and I begin to realise that the role of a parent is to constantly worry about your children. Welcome to the human race indeed.

As she sleeps a lot of the time to begin with, it takes us a day or two to notice that Katie was born with skin tags holding her eyes closed. Each eye has two tiny little pieces of skin, like staples, preventing them from opening up completely. One in the middle, and one at the side of each eye.

The children's eye doctor tells us it's pretty rare and he only sees one or two cases a year. We discover later that Erin actually had the same thing when she was born, and it looks as if this might be the first case ever—that he is aware of—indicating it could be hereditary. He asks our permission to take some pictures, which may well make it into a medical journal. My little lady is already making her mark on the world!

We come back later that day for 'minor' surgery on her eyes, and it is awful. The operation itself is simple, and successful, they just snip the little skin tags—but it's unbelievably distressing to watch. Erin has to leave the room and I just stand there, worrying and watching her cry. Unable to help or do a thing. Helplessness, not a nice feeling.

Then, not long afterwards, one of her eyes begins to weep. They suspect conjunctivitis which is infectious, and until the prognosis is confirmed we have eye drops, and two types of antibiotics injected into her system. Every eight hours we have to take her down into the ICU (intensive care unit). Every four hours something has to be done, either eye drops, flushing the cannula in her tiny wee arm, or taking her down to receive the antibiotics intravenously.

Those trips down into the ICU are sobering though. All those tiny babies in their glass boxes, stressed and tired parents wandering around, unable to even hold and comfort their children. As worried as I am about Katie, I count myself lucky we're not in that situation. Even still, it is pretty draining, emotionally and physically.

Now I understand what my mum has been going through with my sister and I all these years. No wonder she never wanted me to ride a motorbike. No wonder she couldn't stand watching me play rugby. Sorry Mum.

Eventually, the results of Katie's eye swab come back and thankfully she doesn't have conjunctivitis, so they can stop all the antibiotics. She's a little jaundiced however, and they're still keeping a close eye on Erin, so we're not going anywhere in a hurry.

On the up side, we're settling into our new home quite nicely! Getting to know the rhythms of a maternity ward is an experience I certainly didn't expect to stumble across in life, but there you go, and it's actually quite comforting.

Oh, and eventually I find out what the condoms full of frozen water in the freezer are for. Eeyooch, is all I'd like to say about that.

We get to know all the different midwives, the characters, who likes who, and who to watch out for, and the gossip of course—twenty-four hours a day real life drama. But best of all, for that little period of time it's our life support, and our family. Not having any parents over here and without a clue about how to look after a baby, we are soaking up as much information as we can.

Days in and I'm still wandering about in a bit of a dream every time I venture outside. I have now turned into a total sap, and in my head I'm often singing—'Hey Soul Sister' (Train), 'Beautiful Girl' (INXS), 'You're beautiful' (James Blunt). I don't even like that song. Hate the whiney fella, but hey.

Too corny for words, caring not a jot. I find myself looking at these other people out there in the world, listening to the soundtrack in my mind and thinking they don't know—this great secret of mine—I am a father to a beautiful wee girl. I almost feel sorry for them; they have no idea.

It disappears eventually. I don't think the human race would have accepted me back otherwise. Smugness. Horrible. But hey. I'm a new dad!

We take Katie for her first bath a couple of days after she's born, and I'm hit by another fatherly emotion - pride. We're in the room with a wee fella called Benjamin, who's also having his first bath, and he doesn't take to the water too well. He squeals like a little girl, and his mum and grandparents are there to witness his humiliation as my daughter basks calmly in the heat lamp, loving the new experience.

I give him a nickname—Benjamin Bratt, and I feel that little pang of pride, that competitive—'that's my girl'—feeling for the first time ever. Oh dear, I know I'm going to have to watch that, but I'm not sure I'm going to be able to stop it.

Eventually, and unfortunately our little bubble is burst. On day four I'm back to work. We're going to be in hospital for a while, so I decide to keep the rest of my time off until we need it. We'll be on our own soon enough, and I'd rather use my holidays then. Back into the real world. I'm dreading it.

The first day I head back to the office I hesitate, fighting to leave the room as I look at them both lying there in the dark. It's horrible. Once I make it out however I breeze into work and continue to float through the day. New dad.

Proudest man on the planet. Not one of my most productive days at the office I hasten to add.

The rest of the week passes quickly. I'm off to work and home to the postnatal ward at night. They even put a fold down bed in there for me. Erin is getting to know Katie and picking up lots of childcare tips, and then finally, they say— OK, off you go home now, you're fine.

Shit, is my first thought.

16

Home

"We never know the love of a parent until we become parents ourselves."
—Henry Ward Beecher. **Yup, and we find out they didn't have a clue either.**

Walking into the house as a family for the first time is definitely another one of those moments for me. Such contentment and satisfaction, mixed with joy, exhaustion and fear.

I have four more days off work, and half days for two weeks after that, so we can ease into our new life. Actually it's not so bad. We've been in hospital so long that we've picked up the basics—I can change a nappy like a pro; Erin is feeding the wee one, no problem, and the whole sleep thing isn't quite as hard as we were expecting.

It is early days though.

Within a week the first panic arrives. The wee one has a blocked nose and her snuffling just stops. I freak out, more so than Erin I have to admit and eventually, Katie starts breathing again. Probably before me actually, but it is enough to elicit a panicked "What the fuck! How the fuck do you sort that out?! What the fuck?!"

Our main baby book right now is 'Baby Love' by Robin Barker. We use it a lot; in fact, it's invaluable as a point of reference. However I'm in such a state that I forget to even look there for an answer. I just call our friends Melanie and Derek. They have a wee boy about six months old, so I'm hoping they have a solution. And indeed they do. A miniature turkey baster that sucks all the goo out of your baby's nostril. Very effective, but quite an unpleasant experience for everyone involved, they tell me. 'I don't care, better than her not breathing at all. I'm coming to get it.'

It's a gloriously sunny day as I walk along the foreshore to pick up the life saving device for my child. Surely everybody knows. There must be a new father swagger that only comes out on this one particular occasion. A father out for a walk with his baby for the first time. Life don't get much better than that.

I meet up with Mel and Derek, and I can't wipe the smile off my face as I tell them about the events of the last week or so.

The sun was out for me that day, me, Erin and Katie. The rest of the world were just bystanders.

As I write, I feel the emotions welling up again. I remember that little trip very clearly. Lots of things about our first few months at home seemed to blend into one another, but that, I remember.

The first few days back at work full time is knackering, the first full week, exhausting. Now we're getting into it.

We do have a little help to begin with. Erin's sister Niamh is great; Sophie and James drop round occasionally, make us dinner then leave. Perfect. Just what we need. Then we have a few other friends round to 'see the baby' one weekend, and it's not at all what I am expecting.

They arrive and I am excited to see them all – excited to show off our beautiful wee girl. There is a very brief 'Ooh, there she is,' and then that's it. The chat goes straight onto what happened over the weekend, who had been out where—how drunk they'd all been, who had a dreadful hangover—blah, blah, blah.

I couldn't give a flying fuck. Boozing, trailing around bars and all the rest of it, I'm not part of that anymore, and it seems somehow… shallow. We have a bite to eat on the balcony and they leave.

I'm absolutely gutted. I'm so excited about this new wee person who has entered into the world, and these friends of mine couldn't give a shit.

Oh how life changes. We have someone to look after other than ourselves. Someone who completely and utterly depends on us for everything in life. Someone for whom I would willingly give my life, my last penny, my all.

They just have hangovers and careless stories.

It did go away eventually, that feeling of self-righteousness and general disgust with the rest of the world, but at that point, everything that everybody else was doing just seemed pointless; self-indulgent.

Funny though, I remember being in the same situation myself a few years back; I was the one visiting a new-born and the proud parents – and no doubt doing exactly the same as my 'hung over' friends had done that day.

Ah, the irony. It wasn't long before I was longing for a shallow and self-indulgent night out on the town.

After my first full week back at work, Niamh comes to stay with us for a while.

Once again she is a great help, and it's during this time I have my first few evenings on my own in a room with Katie, while she screams at the top of her lungs. Oh. My. God.

How in the hell can anything so small make such an unbelievably loud noise? Here I am working ridiculously hard, not sleeping enough – and coming home to near continuous screaming every night, or so it seems. Talk about settling in.

Niamh manages to drag me to the cinema and we watch any old crap—something with Mark Wahlberg in it, take your pick. After longing for a break from everything, it's only half an hour into the movie before I find myself wondering how they're getting on, how they're doing without me. 'Is this it?' I think. 'Am I fucked for movies now too?'

We go for a pint afterwards, and as I sit in the pub sipping Guinness I'm not much for conversation. Still a little shell-shocked perhaps, and the Guinness tastes fan-fuckin-tastic.

Aside from the screaming, there are the odd, quiet little moments, with just me and Katie. I watch her stretch. I watch her face. Watch her instant reaction to whatever she is feeling. Despite what many people had said—that babies don't 'give you much' as a father for the first few months—I find watching her expressions amazing. They are so pure, instantly going from pleasure, to pain, to calm….whatever. So honest.

Not everybody would notice the subtle changes I'm sure, but I'll bet everybody notices them in their own child. Total sap. Instantly.

Later, when Erin read what I'd written about these early experiences—the joys and pleasures of new-found fatherhood—she remarked how different they were to hers. Not that she wasn't happy, but the overwhelming feeling for her, from birth throughout the first six months or so, was tiredness. Closely followed by stress.

And while I was no stranger to either of these, they weren't as all consuming for me as they were for her. Not that you shouldn't be happy or give yourself over to the experience, just be aware that your partner is probably carrying a bit more than you are.

And it could be worth doing whatever you can to alleviate the load. I think I did alright on that front. And while the results of my assistance were maybe not always the most successful, Erin says she wouldn't give me anything less than an A for effort.... or at least an A-.

17

One Month: A Different World

"As a father you don't really get that much out of the first few months."
—Idiots. **What a load of bollox.**

Labour day, Monday off work. A long weekend when I discover that Foxtel is a load of shite, and I am a total lightweight.

I come home early on Friday with a bottle of wine. We order takeaway Thai to mark the weekend, as seems to be the routine at the moment.

Foxtel was installed during the week so we're going to chill, watch TV, maybe make a den in the living room, lounge around and relax.

That was the plan anyway, but as 5pm rolls around I just hit the wall. I feel as if I've been in a fight. My shoulder is absolutely agony, my mouth is sore, my stomach's not great, so I take myself off to bed.

I'm up again about 8pm, so I've had 3 hours sleep before the dream feed, then I manage another 11 hours afterwards. Pretty good going. It's a bit embarrassing actually, I'm getting more sleep in general than Erin is, and she's doing a lot better than me. Man flu maybe. Although I'm sure there must be some hormones at work in Erin's body to help her keep going.

I thought I'd been managing better recently too, but I guess not. I must have really needed that 11-hour stretch. Katie screamed for an hour and a half this morning and I didn't hear a thing.

So we didn't build a den, and Foxtel seems to be just endless repeats. Episodes of the Housewives of wherever the fuck, the freakin' Kardashians and Guliana & Bill or some other eejits.

But I do get to spend a lot of time with Katie, which is brilliant. Erin heads out to the shops and the two of us just hang out for a good couple of hours on our own.

It sure is a different world nowadays.

This is how it's all playing out.

Basically, Katie needs to be fed every three hours, and everything else revolves around that.

After a feed, there's about 20 minutes of awake time. She's alert, receptive to what's going on and it is really the only chance to interact with her. Then it's time for her to go back down to sleep. Apart from those 20 minutes, she's either feeding or sleeping, you're trying to feed her, or you're trying to get her to sleep. And the last thing you want to do to a baby that you're trying to get to sleep, is talk to her. There's lots of shushing and patting, but certainly no discussions, no room for chit-chat.

You're looking for that first yawn, and once you see it you've got to move quickly, get her wrapped, quieten her down then get her off to bed. It's back to windows again. This is your opportunity. If you miss it, she gets over tired and it's a nightmare. Instead of taking 10–30 minutes to get her down to sleep, it can take you up to an hour. And there will be screaming.

Thing is, if it takes you an hour to get her down to sleep, it's not long until she's up again, hungry, and it starts all over again. Groundhog day, except every three hours, 24 hours a day.

I can understand how people lose their minds trying to get a little bit of peace and quiet. Especially if they don't have any support around them. Someone to come in and take the baby off your hands for a couple of hours. Katie isn't quite that bad, but she's not that great either.

During the week, my time with her is at the 11 o'clock feed. It's known as the 'dream feed', and basically I preempt her waking up crying and hungry by giving her a bottle while she's half asleep. Babies are driven very much by instinct, so as soon as I put that bottle in her mouth, she starts sucking on it. The dream feed buys Erin a six hour break from the ritual. Although I'm never very happy getting up at 11pm, once I get going it's a lovely, quiet part of the evening.

I go to sleep around 10pm, then get up at 11pm. Get her out of the bassinette, change her nappy and then we sit on the couch as I give her roughly 100ml of milk, which takes around 20–25 minutes. She'd take it quicker if I let her but then she throws up—so I have to split it up, pull the bottle out of her wee mouth to force a break and wind her in between courses.

To do this I sit her up on my left leg, put a hand on her chest, and a hand on her back. Her eyes bug out a little, arms straight, fingers asplay, little Winston Churchill chubby cheeks. Then, with a bit of luck, as I rub her back we get a burp. I lay her down on my right leg, rub the back some more as her arms hang over towards the couch. We might get another burp and then it's back to my lap for more food. Bottle finished, I wrap her, and rub her front for 20 minutes before putting her down to sleep again.

I read a book for this last part, as I rub, making sure she is in a deep sleep. I'm sure I'm doing my eyes some damage reading in the dark like this, but hey.

I finish *Long Way Down* by Ewan McGregor and Charlie Boorman, and then move onto *Mafia* by A.G.D. Maran.

Usually when I read a travel book like that I feel restless and want to head off somewhere, but sitting there in my living room with a tiny person in my lap, I'm as happy as Larry.

I get to look straight into her eyes. Sometimes she looks back, sometimes she's staring intently at her bottle, sometimes she's just taking it all in and occasionally she closes her eyes, and falls asleep. As she's sitting there in my lap, she's all mine, and I love it.

I did the dream feed every night for about eight or nine months. It was frequently frustrating, but I still look back on it as a special time for Katie and I.

Overall life was pretty sweet then, although the lack of sleep was a bit of a shock to the system and Erin and I were a bit short with each other sometimes. It's a long day at home on your own with a baby, and when I came home from work late on the odd occasion, I think the cold reception I sometimes received was because she'd been so looking forward to seeing me. Nothing out of the ordinary I'm sure.

Katie even got herself off to sleep on her own sometimes, once you'd spent a while calming her down that was.

I am particularly enjoying our alone time, although I do have to stop my mind from wandering on the odd occasion. Sitting there trying to feed her, or trying to get her to sleep I find myself going through a mental to-do list, and when I catch myself at it—I stop.

I try to be mindful of the moment, to appreciate just being there with my daughter, rather than thinking about all the other things that need my attention. There will be time for that later, and if she was gone tomorrow, what would I rather have spent my time doing?

18

Two Months: Sleep Deprivation Dreams

> *"No matter what you've done for yourself or for humanity, if you can't look back on having given love and attention to your family, what have you really accomplished?"*
> —Elbert Hubbart. **Probably quite a lot!**

These are now the most important questions in life. How's the little one eating? How's she sleeping? Is she well? And they're all inextricably linked. If a baby is eating well, most likely they're sleeping a lot too. Which means that they're A—OK and you're probably cruising along wondering what all the fuss was about. Or, you'll get the flip side, which means not a lot of eating, not a lot of sleep, and trouble all around.

Katie was probably somewhere in the middle, but we didn't know that at the time.

She was eating OK (or drinking really) but she would cry immediately afterwards. Even when I gave her the odd bottle, she'd often be crying throughout the process, only stopping when I had the bottle in her mouth, and as soon as it was out—back to the crying. Most babies don't do this, but we didn't know that either. We were told by the midwives who visited now and again that babies just cry a lot, and that's that.

She was an absolute delight though, and no matter how much crying there is, I would challenge any new parent not to be completely amazed by their new wee person.

She has started giving us the odd smile now too, and it just makes my day when she smiles at me. She is pretty stingy with them though, doesn't dole them out willy-nilly. Most of the time she seems to be quite a thoughtful baby.

Apart from the crying that is... crying non-stop for two hours at the top of her lungs doesn't seem like a very thoughtful act, although it puts a few in my mind. "When in God's name will this end?" and of course "What have I gotten myself into!?" Two hours is quite extreme though, she's not normally that upset for that length of time.

She is also still very small, and most other babies the same age seem massive. Yet she is strong. She's been holding her neck up for weeks, no problem, where most other babies can't do that yet. Granted most other baby's heads are twice the size but nevertheless... Ah that fatherly pride again... poor ol' Benjamin Bratt freaking out when he got his feet wet for the first time. Ha! Big girl's blouse.

And although she is small, she *is* still growing. It's just that you don't notice it. When I look back at pictures from only a month ago, I can really tell the difference, it's amazing how much she's changed.

One of the frightening things, apart from the fact that we actually have a real live baby of our own (and that her hair has a little ginger tinge to it) is the fact that it all seems to be happening so quickly. It's almost sad. We both sort of want her to stay at this age forever, because she's so beautiful and perfect. Parenthood... does funny things I'm telling you. Not the least of which is the fact that we can't be bothered going out anymore either. And I mean, not at all. At least no further than a couple of blocks. I used to wonder why people just disappeared when they had a kid? Now I know. I'm just not interested in the rest of the world anymore. I feel that this wee family is all that matters. Who needs other people? Fuck 'em.

We try to keep our weekends quiet, finding one 'outing' enough. And if we are out for too long, it just throws Katie off her sleep, her routine, and that is a real pain in the ass. It is definitely easier if people come to see us. What we enjoy the most right now, is just chilling out at home on our own, lounging around for half the day doing nothing. Well, looking after Katie certainly isn't nothing, but it's great to have no commitments, to go back to sleep ourselves in the afternoon if we feel like it, do whatever. Wander around in my underpants all day. Not *that* much different from usual then. Just less empty pizza boxes lying around.

Wetting the baby's head

One outing I am looking forward to is my 'wetting the baby's head' night.

In Scotland, it's usually done on the actual night of the birth. Your missus will most likely be in hospital, well looked after—so you'll call round your mates, tell them you're a dad and everyone meets up in the pub for a few beers. In the movies this is when they're handing out cigars to all and sundry—and I've been to a few like that. I've been to some that lasted well into the early hours of the next morning, and I've been to a few that were more reasonable—home when the pub closes. Back in Scotland it doesn't matter what night of the week it is, when you make that call, your friends gather together, and it's beers and whisky all round.

It's a wee bit different in Australia. It seems to happen a few months after the big day, and I must admit I'm not a fan.

I had a couple of beers with my sister in law, Niamh, on the night of the birth, and my official 'wetting the baby's head night' is well into the third month of it all. On the birth night, even if you're exhausted and maybe a little spaced out like I was, the emotions are still so raw. It's fresh, and exciting, and the very brink of your new life as a father. It's *just* the time to be with your mates.

A few months later, you're fairly well removed from all of that. And gathering together with a few pals for some beers is nice, but it's not quite the same. You're also fairly well ensconced in your new life by then, so you know fine well that you can't really cut loose if you want to. Because you know what it's like now. You know that your sleep is precious, and you know that a hangover is the very last thing you want when a wee baby is around.

Nevertheless I have an enjoyable evening on my official night. I get the train straight into town after work, and it feels odd not going directly home. I come out of the station at Circular Quay, amazed at all the people out and about. I haven't seen so many people in ages. Real people, going about their lives. Woo hoo! A few beers with the guys, head home and tucked up in bed before midnight. Respectable. Erin gives me a bit of a lie in the next day, taking Katie out in the morning to give me a break. Wetting the baby's head—tick.

If I was offering advice on the matter—I'd say try and do it within the first few days, certainly before your missus and your kid return home from hospital. After that, it's a different ball game. I would also highly recommend giving your partner a bit of grace the day after a bevy, or it's just not worthwhile. I know of people who have to get right into it the following morning, no matter what. If that was the case with me, I wouldn't bother going out at all.

Routine, routine, routine

I remember my mum asking when I was a kid, "What do you want to eat next Tuesday?" or something equally stupid like that. I used to hate those questions and would invariably whine my reply, "I don't know, ask me next Tuesday". What a dick.

Now I know what that was all about. In fact my mum was being nice even asking instead of just serving it up. It's routine. Now I know how important routine is. For a baby it's everything, and to run a household, essential.

A baby needs routine to function properly, and if you want your life to do the same, you have to respect that. There are two schools of thought involved here. You either let the baby do whatever the hell she likes, eat, sleep whenever and wherever (basically find her own routine) or you attempt to impose some form of control—and try to bring her habits and routine into line with yours. Neither way is best necessarily, it's just whatever works for you, and your baby. If you're trying to hold down a job for example, having your baby sleep at night is kind of useful. There's an unbelievable amount of literature about this subject, and we read a good bit of it, but no baby is a text book baby—you just keep trying things until they work. Good luck. Anyway, routine.

This is an average week right now.

Mondays and Wednesdays I start work at 7am. This allows me to leave at 4pm, arriving home early enough to see Katie before she gets crabby and difficult to deal with.

Sometimes there are house chores to do, but most of the time I just head home and play with Katie. 'Tummy time' is big just now, basically putting Katie on her front so she can exercise her stomach muscles trying to look up.

Erin and I generally have a chat, and we'll talk to Katie as if she knows what we're saying. I used to think that people who did this were eejits. Now I know it's a way of stimulating your child, getting them used to your voice and can actually be soothing for them too. I even sing to her sometimes. My old self would be disgusted with the person I've turned into. But hey, I don't really give a shit. Now and again I also try and make 'obvious' faces—a huge big smile—a frown, to see if she can copy them. Not too sure if she follows me with that though, maybe it's just wishful thinking.

We play with Katie for a while and then I'll nurse her and put her down around 5:30pm. She'll sleep for about 30 to 45 minutes, then up for another feed from her mother at 7pm. It takes quite a while to get her back to sleep after this one—but once it's done we'll eat ourselves, and generally go straight to bed. With a bit of luck we're in bed for 9:30pm, I'll get an hour's kip before I'm up for the dream feed at 10:30/11pm—which used to take about 1 hour 15 minutes from start to finish. I've managed to get it down to 45 minutes now. She's up again at 3am, then again around 6am, and then we're into the next day.

That's how it goes on Mondays and Wednesdays, and pretty much most of the week, except I don't have time to play with Katie on Tuesdays, Thursdays and Fridays.

On those days it is straight into the crying as soon as I walk in the door. I hear it as I walk up the stairs of the apartment block. I'll stand outside the door and compose myself before I head in—a few deep breaths—and into it. I'll take her from Erin and sit on the bed in our room, holding her, while she cries and eventually calms down. She generally cries for an hour every evening. It's fine, but I do prefer my early days when I get to spend some time with her before the tears start.

As I've said, we're not really into doing that much at the weekends anymore, but I've started trying to do a regular sit down dinner on a Sunday, and I'll take Katie out on my own most weekends at some point too—to give Erin a break. On Sunday nights now and again, I'll sleep in the back room for a much needed, uninterrupted night's sleep. And that's a week with a 2-month old.

Talking of sleep

Another thing I'm aware of now, is the reason they use sleep deprivation as a form of torture. If you're not getting enough of it, you'll sell your soul for a single night's peace. "911 Iain, we know you were involved" "Aye, sure, was all me, the whole fucking lot, now let me go to sleep for fuck sake." "You're aware that the penalty is life imprisonment?" "Aye, good, now fuck off."

I am still tired a lot of the time but not as knackered as I was in the first few weeks, and it's nowhere near as bad as I was expecting it to be, Nevertheless my coffee consumption has increased dramatically. I'm up to about eight cups a day (from probably one or two previously) and I don't think I'd be able to get through a day's work without it.

Katie does sleep through the night on a couple of occasions, from 10:30pm—7am, but she doesn't make a habit of it. And Erin is constantly up, making sure she is still alive so even then, we aren't sleeping through ourselves.

One night I get up to do the dream feed and it feels like the most difficult thing I've ever done in my life. I don't want to see anyone, do anything, just sleep. Torture... I understand how people just head off for a pint of milk and never come back.

Number two

That being the case, I almost surprise *myself* by being the first to mention baby number two. Not even three months into it and I'm talking about the next one. Not that I want another kid straight away, but I *am* the first one to bring it up in conversation. How about that? Oh how the thought processes change.

When you've left it late like we have though, you can't hang around for too long, or you're not supposed to anyway. I'd like Katie to have a friend as she grows up and it would be nice to have a wee group of us as a family. And if anything ever happened to Erin and I... doesn't bear thinking about.

I'm six years older than my sister, and although I was just that wee bit too old for us to be into the same things at the same time, we were generally great pals. We fought like fury on the odd occasion of course, but we've always been there for each other—no matter what's going on. And when you get a bit older, the age gap virtually disappears anyway.

I do think that having a brother or a sister adds another dimension to your life. A valuable, enriching one, and it's something I would like Katie to have eventually, as much as it pains me to say it right now. Erin's one of six of course, and needs no convincing of the love and laughter that comes from a family full of people. Although at this point in time? Fwhoo... Not now. No way.

At the moment. I can hardly even believe we have one kid, never mind two. Sometimes I feel like I'm going to wake up, and find out it was a dream.

Not where I'd pictured myself, but then again what a ride, what an experience, what an adventure. Amazing how much life changes, and so much for the better. Not that there was anything wrong before, but after—it's just, different. Number two, Jesus. Fairly sure I scared the shit out of Erin too.

How to stop a baby crying: Facts of life
If you knew the answer to this the world would be yours for the taking. There are lots of things to try, but none are foolproof. It also depends on how old your child is.

Here's a list. Best to just work your way through until you find something that works. Bear in mind you might not find anything that does the trick. Still, better at least to try something, as opposed to doing nothing and slowly losing your mind.

—Feed them
—Change their nappy
—Cuddle them
—Try a rocking type motion
—Walk around while cuddling them
—Take them into a dark room and cuddle them
—Take them outside and cuddle them
—Tell them to shut the fuck up

19

Three Months: Throw In A Hand Grenade

"We're getting on just fine, no change at all."
— Smug new parents. **Bullshit.**

It's not all sweetness and light, though. Mostly, yes, but there's also the stresses and strains that come from two people living together under a good bit more pressure than they're used to. Throw in a bit of sleep deprivation and worry, and you're going to get on each other's nerves now and again.

I remember reading somewhere that having a baby is like throwing a hand grenade into a relationship. It's pretty accurate. You've got to be in a fairly robust partnership I'd say, to manage through. These people who have a kid to save their marriage?! Not that I know any myself, but you hear the stories. I can't imagine anything worse for two people who *already* aren't getting on.

It's just little things. For example, let's talk about house chores. Even before you throw a baby into the picture, when two people are living under one roof there are tons of little things you have to learn to do, if you want to avoid strangling each other.

You know the thing, put the dishes in the dishwasher, not just in the sink. And when you do put them in the dishwasher, give them a good clean before you do so. You know, that sort of shit. There are layers of these things that you just pick up and get on with, no big deal. And being a bloke, I'm not always the best at remembering them all.

Well, there's a shit load more of these tasks that arrive with a baby. And that's puttin' it mildly. They change on a daily basis too, so pay attention, you've got to keep up. Most make sense, but they're hard to keep a handle on and you constantly forget.

These are the sorts of things that drive people crazy. Especially when you're being tortured with exhaustion. Little annoyances can be magnified, and blown out of all proportion.

Another factor that doesn't help the situation, as I've already mentioned, is that I don't like being told what to do. Nobody does, I would imagine, but I seem to have something deep down inside of me that just says 'No, fuck off' whenever someone tries to order me around. It might be part of being Scottish (maybe it's a Glaswegian thing) and I reckon it's why I've found it difficult to work for other people. Also, probably, why I don't like bossy people, people who think they know everything, and… yeah there are quite a few segments of society I'd love to tell to fuck off.

Anyway. When you're with a baby, maybe trying to put them down or feeding them, you're fairly limited in the number of other tasks you can undertake at that point in time. You're often restricted in how far you can move for example, without upsetting the kid and sending yourself back to square one again. Very frustrating.

So if there's someone else around, it's pretty handy. That's just the way it is. And you want to help out in any way you can (because you feel so goddamn guilty about being at work all day while your missus does all the heavy lifting?). Whatever the reasons, you'll do what's required.

However, sometimes, if you're knackered, and if you've had a bad day at work for whatever reason, the manner in which you've been asked might really piss you off.

It might sound more like an order, than a request.

"Go and put the bottles in the dishwasher."

"Get me a towel. No, not *that* towel, that one over there."

Normally not an issue at all, you wouldn't even notice it—or you'd say something back in jest. But given this new situation that you're in, where everyone is still trying to find their way, little things can be fucking huge for a while.

A Glaswegian's perspective? Hmm… I think it's bigger than that, pretty sure the majority of males don't respond well to orders in general.

Anyway, it's something that I have to become aware of in myself, and try to manage my reaction to. Because sometimes the slight, or demand, is more imagined than real. Simply a request lost in translation amidst the stress and exhaustion. It's just life, but with a new wee person on board.

It does change the dynamic of your relationship though, and people who say that life is carrying on as before are either incredibly lucky with their child, or lying—maybe even to themselves.

There's definitely a period of adjustment to the new reality. And how easily it's all going, determines how long the adjustment period lasts. It's not always going to go smoothly, but then again most things that are worthwhile require a bit of hard work.

I'm also beginning to see how easy it might be to become just a couple of people managing a project—which happens to be your child. How easy it would be to start taking each other for granted, and lose touch with each other. There's so much to organise, so much to do and it *can* become all about the logistics. We do try and create time for the two of us—

and we're doing alright, up to a point. There *is* a life outside of the baby, we just have to remind ourselves now and again.

The end of the third month is a milestone in a child's development. Three months down. Phew, you've made it. Getting pregnant for a start, not as easy as you might have thought. Through the pregnancy, in our case not quite as bad as we expected. The birth—traumatizing, the first three months—hard work—and now, at the end of the third month—if your kid hasn't been sleeping through the night yet, this is when it's supposed to kick in.

Unfortunately for us, it's beginning to look a bit like the birth plan all over again. Take the gel, go to sleep, wake up and have a baby, finished in time for dinner and a good night's sleep for everyone. Oh yeah? Pfft. It just doesn't seem to be heading that way. Sleep. Hmm. I remember that…

I was soon to learn that hanging out for a particular developmental sign was the road to ruin—so I'm not going to get into them too much from here on in. Consult another book for that, at your peril. But if you do, remember, every baby is different. There are NO text book babies. If your kid reaches ten and all they can say is daddy then you may have a problem, but you don't need a fuckin' book to tell you that. Beware.

20

Four Months: It's All I Can Remember

"Grandparents adore their grandkids; they know that they can give them back soon."
— David Cuschieri. **Aye, can see that.**

I can hardly remember what life was like before Katie. Yet these first four months have flown, and suddenly here's Christmas. Time off, time to relax, and time for the first overseas family visit.

Niamh and I pick up Bernie and Deirdre, Erin's mum and another sister, at the airport on Boxing Day, and we're all excited for them to meet Katie for the first time. We are so proud of our wee girl and we're just dying for family to meet her.

We arrive back at the apartment and there is, as expected, calamity. As I mentioned before, Erin comes from quite a large family (two brothers and four sisters) and when they were growing up, I think they all had to shout in order to be heard over the racket going on in the house. So you can imagine the noise when they all get back together again now—never mind the fact that there's a new baby in the picture.

Shouting, laughter, Katie passed around and cheered—she absolutely loves it.

I recede into the background and wait for everyone to calm down. It takes a while, but eventually we are all settled down with cups of tea, biscuits and sandwiches on the go – very Irish.

So, I think. Can I have my daughter back please? But no, there are other people in the picture now, and they all want a piece of her. Within minutes, I have become surplus to requirements. Our little self-sustaining family unit has some new members. All of a sudden we're a clan, and the roles that Erin and I are only just getting used to, change.

Taking some time out
Over the next two weeks I have some time to myself I haven't been expecting. I go surfing, diving, I play golf and to begin with I feel so incredibly selfish. How could I be out here in the world doing something that is only for my own gratification, while my little family is at home without me…I can see how you could end up devoting your entire life to these wee people, and have trouble getting back to normal 18 years later when they bugger off. 'Now, where was I? What was I doing? Who the fuck am I?'.

I soon get back into it though. It's nice having some time to do 'normal' things again, and it is great having family around for a while. It also helps to get us out more often. After they leave, we're a bit more interested in the real world again. Well maybe it's just me. Erin hasn't gone into hibernation quite as much as I have, but anyway—it's a good thing to get out more.

And then it's my birthday. Another change from the 'old' days before Katie came along—it is a much quieter affair than in the past. What makes the day for me is that Erin and Katie come to my work to join me for lunch in the lobby.

I couldn't be happier. Katie has started giving me a bit of cold shoulder lately, so getting to see them at lunchtime will hopefully sort that out. A day at the office, lunch with Erin and Katie and I run home from work. Without the work bit, it would have been a perfect day.

Not such a perfect day for Katie however, as we give her Formula for the first time. She's been used to the good stuff up until now, mother's milk from the source or the bottle—and I'm the one to introduce her to the alternative later on that evening. She doesn't like it one little bit, won't take it at all to begin with. I see this look in her eye, as she peers up at me as if to say, "What the fuck is this buddy!?".

I consider it her first lesson in life, and I find it a little bit sad letting my wee girl know that unfortunately, you can't always get what you want. The Stones play in my head as I persist and she eventually takes a drink.

We take her to the swimming pool for the first time too, so I feel as if that makes up for it. I'm very much a water person, I love swimming, surfing, sailing, diving—pretty much anything that gets me next to, near, or in the water so this is a big thing for me. Much to my relief, she absolutely loves it. She is a brave wee girl as she's splashed by some annoying kids in the pool—no tears at all—although I could do with giving those little buggers something to cry about.

So, swimming a success, and I can already picture the two of us surfing somewhere up the coast and diving the Great Barrier Reef together.

You see sweetheart, you *can't* always get what you want, but on the odd occasion something you never expected turns up, and it's wonderful.

21

Five Months: Now We're Getting Into It

"I take my children everywhere, but they always find their way back home."
—Robert Oren. **Ah, yup.**

January is a great time of year in Australia. The weather's usually beautiful. You get loads of time off over Christmas, and as you return to work and attempt to summon up some enthusiasm for the coming year, you're rewarded with another day off, Australia Day.

The next Grandparent to visit is my dad, due to arrive Australia Day, and we have a carefully planned week ahead of us starting with a picnic in a local park. Unfortunately his flight from Bangkok is turned around after flying for only a couple of hours. Engine problems. Qantas. Surprise, surprise. Everyone ends up in an airport hotel for 24 hours before getting back on the same plane, and taking off for Sydney again. A few of them none too happy due to an unfortunate glimpse of the replacement engine while it was strapped to the roof of another jet!

This sort of thing always seems to happen to my dad. He regularly stumbles into unusual and often hilarious situations. Here's one: My dad runs a golfing business in Thailand, arranging competitions on occasion for corporate clients and their guests. There was a particularly extravagant affair not that long ago, where a load of Chinese businessmen toured the country accompanied by an enormous entourage, one of whom was my dad.

He was set up at a little table in the lobby of a five star resort in Phuket, waiting for the guests to register for the competition, when he was informed that they'd been held up. It was the head of the entourage who told him this, and he just happened to have six of the hotel's masseuses, booked out for the next couple of hours. Their time was bought and paid for, so, he asked if my dad would mind waiting in the reception a bit longer while six Thai ladies massaged his back and shoulders. Well who's going to argue with that!? And of course, two minutes later an old friend of his happens to walk into the lobby. "Fuck me Harry, what are you the King of bloody Phuket now!" See what I mean? I don't know anyone else who stumbles into that kind of shit.

When he finally arrives we are regaled with the story of the trip, as he and Katie get acquainted. She seems fascinated by his hair, which is short, kind of spiky, and silver grey. Thankfully she warms to him, frequently giving up her big smiles.

I'd heard a few of the stories from my childhood before, and knew that I was a bit of a terror, but now I had a kid myself, my dad, of course, starts to recount them anew. And hearing them now as a parent, is horrifying. Most frightening of all is the fact that I didn't sleep through the night until I was six. Six years that is. Oh, my, God…

I was a hyperactive little fellow, always running about causing trouble, never still unless we were out having dinner somewhere. It appears I had the ability to hold it all in when I wanted to, and often people would approach my mum and dad in restaurants to comment on my good manners. They quietly smiled and said thanks, hoping that I wouldn't start throwing things around or climbing up the walls before the nice people left.

Oh yeah, Dad couldn't wait for a bit of payback. And with sleep being a real problem for Katie just now, I'm sure he was relishing the universal justice of it all.

He recalled one particular holiday in Malta, when I was up at the crack of dawn every day. I would run up and down the room, and then the corridor, and eventually he had to remove me from the hotel to avoid us all being told to leave. He'd throw me, then a packet of biscuits into the pram (buying a temporary reprieve as I devoured them) and then he huckled me out of there. We'd walk around the old port and he was on first name terms with the local fishermen by the end of the holiday.

My mum recalls he promised to thump me when I reached 18, telling me "That was for Malta". Hmmm….

So, as I was saying about Katie and her sleep—it's now beginning to rule our lives, even more so than before. She sleeps at night reasonably well, only up a couple of times which is perfectly acceptable. But during the day, problems are really starting to kick in.

It's all back to the eating—sleeping—all is well with the world cycle. A kid at this age is supposed to be eating every four hours or so, sleeping for about 45 minutes, and at lunchtime they should be able to tack two of these 45-minute sleeping sessions together, giving everyone a blissful hour and a half hour off.

Time to tidy up, organise your life or go back to sleep yourself. Sleep is the option we're favouring, being fairly frazzled most of the time. Everything else in life has taken a distinct back seat and tidying up seems to be about the only other thing I ever do.

The problem is that Katie still doesn't eat that much, and when she does, there is about an hour of seriously loud crying afterwards, then a bit of sleep, then back into it again. I think she eventually sleeps at night because she is so knackered. Who isn't?

When you're continuously faced with the repetitiveness of it all, the loud crying and lack of sleep situation, you'll do anything for it to stop. If you ever find yourself going through this you have my sympathy, it's a nightmare.

There is hope however. As you'll realise by now, there's no end to the number of 'baby help' books out there. So called super-mums who've done it all and have the answers to your woes. These books give you hope. Sometimes they might even work, but I wouldn't bet on it.

Generally they all promote their own 'technique' that promises a baby who sleeps, eats, does all the right things, blah, blah, blah... the two options that seem to dominate however, are controlled crying, and PUPD (Pick Up Put Down).

Controlled crying is where you allow them to cry in the cot for a certain period of time, say two minutes, then you go in, comfort them with a pat or two and some shooshing, then leave the room. If they keep crying, you go in again after a slightly longer period of time, then longer, then longer... and eventually, they're supposed to get the picture that you're there for them, but they'll have to learn how to comfort and settle themselves down to sleep. That's the idea anyway. We can't quite bring ourselves to sit there while she is crying however, so we choose the other route.

A friend who had been through some sleeping issues with her children recommends a book called 'The Baby Whisperer'. It expounds the virtues of PUPD, and on the odd occasion we see a bit of improvement, but nothing lasting.

Our course is set however, and so for the sake of sanity (or what is left of it)—we have to stay with the program.

With PUPD, you go in after they've been crying for 30 seconds, hold them to your chest for a quick comfort, and immediately put them back down again. Then you wait. Right there by the cot. If they start crying again, pick 'em up after 30 seconds of wailing, quick comfort, then down again. Repeat, repeat, repeat, repeat—until you want to kill yourself, your child, or anyone who just happens to be passing by.

I do this frequently for an hour non-stop, and on one occasion when it lasts for an hour and a half, I actually fantasise about running out of the room with Katie and throwing her off the balcony. We're one floor up and there's a pool out there—whether I'd be able to launch her in to the pool or not is irrelevant. Couldn't care less.

As bad as it is for me, I only get this at the weekends. Erin is faced with it every single day—and not only is her patience, sanity, and tolerance being tested, her back is beginning to suffer too. All that bloody bending down and straightening up from the cot. Then she reaches her 'I'm at the end of my tether' moment.

This is our life when my dad arrives, so while he is most likely enjoying a bit of payback (I never did get thumped for that Malta trip) he does feel for us too.

On reflection we've both agreed there's no way we'd do the PUPD again. We had a baby who was sleeping through the night, reasonably well at least, only up just the normal two to three times. And to be creating these problems for ourselves during the day because Katie wasn't sleeping as much as the 'books' say she should have been? Crazy…but you never know, to begin with it's all so new—you just do what you think is right at the time, and hope for the best.

Another time I'm in the middle of an hour long, back punishing PUPD routine. Katie wailing, big round face, big round mouth. 'Waaaagh, Waaaaaagh,' just the usual for a Sunday afternoon, except that right in the middle of it I do an enormous fart, and she laughs!

For a fraction of a second, the corners of her mouth turn upwards. Definitely not a grimace, a real smile, and then she laughs, then the wailing resumes. Brilliant! I find it hilarious of course, and to me this is irrefutable evidence that farts are funny. It's not toilet humour, it's not childish, it's not learned behaviour, it's genetic, inbuilt and deep down. Farts are funny. Case closed.

At least I can thank PUPD for that.

Erin and my dad spend quite a lot of time together with Katie during the trip, unable to leave the house for too long because of the bloody sleep situation, but my dad is cool with it, and it is a real pleasure having him around for a while.

We had planned to visit an old family friend in Port Stephens (about two and a half hours up the coast) but when the time comes, the thought of being in someone else's house with all that's going on is just too much. Plus the little lady doesn't like the car, and we've not been able to go more than 20 minutes without her starting to bawl at the top of her lungs. So the trip would be a freakin' nightmare. In the end, at Erin's insistence, Dad and I go up on our own.

It is the first time I've been away since Katie was born, and I feel terribly guilty cruising up the Pacific Highway, away from my life as it has become. It is also quite exciting though, I must admit. I feel like I've been set free, from the PUPD at least anyway. A road trip! Just like Erin and I used to do all the time. It's good to spend a few hours with my dad too, although he drifts off to sleep now and again - kind of like Katie really, but with less crying.

Dad's trip comes and goes quickly however, and here we are still banging away at the bloody PUPD. We decide it's OK to throw in the towel now though. We've been at it for long enough, we've given it a chance and it hasn't worked. In a 'fuck this I've had enough' moment, I grab a card that is stuck on the fridge for some kind of nanny, picked up at a doctor's or in a hospital somewhere, and call the number.

"Hello, super nanny? We're fucked. Can you help us out? Can you come round tonight? Good let's get on with it…oh, wait a minute, how much do you charge? What? Fuck. Ahh, OK, come on round, let's get it done."

That's maybe not *exactly* how the conversation goes but it's not a million miles away. It's about $900, and I promise you, if you ever reach this stage, you will gladly pay twice that to sort it all out.

When she arrives we are ecstatic about the prospect of a normal, sleeping baby. And she certainly looks the part, wearing all the Victorian nanny gear it seems as if she was born into the profession. We call her Nanny McPhee.

Her technique is her own version of controlled crying, and by now we have no qualms at all about letting the little terrorist cry for a while on her own—well, I certainly haven't. Erin leaves the house for a couple of hours, and we get to work.

After a good few hours of in and out, lots of crying, a CD of white noise and a bit of chit-chat in between, we finally have a baby who sleeps. Why on earth did we wait so long? The indomitable Miss McPhee says to call her whenever we like over the next couple of weeks. If we need any more advice, or help, she's only a phone call away. And that's it, done.

I show her to the door, and there's a guy I don't know in the corridor of the apartment building as I say cheerio. He is mid 20s, wearing a blue blazer with a pink shirt and shiny cufflinks, a finance wanker who thinks he rules the world.

He looks at this rather unorthodox woman as if she's just crawled out of the drain. 'How dare you even address me' in his look, and I'm struck with an almost overwhelming desire to pummel his face into a bloody mess. I seriously have to hold myself back. A total stranger! I don't care. In just that one look, there is such disdain it makes my blood boil.

Fair enough, she did look a little unusual in her old fashioned garb—but hey, so what, she's Nanny McPhee, and she's just saved our lives! Who the fuck does he think he is?! Amazing how such strong emotions can be elicited so quickly sometimes. I'm not normally like this I promise.

I write this in my diary the next day:

'My advice to my daughter. Stay away from assholes—those fuckers who look down their noses at everyone. People like that actually don't care about anyone else in the world, that's what to look out for really, whether someone actually gives a shit about other people or not.'

The new regime works for about five days. Then my mum arrives from Scotland, it works for another couple of days after that, then that's it. $900 for seven days peace. Worth every penny.

Valentine's day

I hate Valentine's Day. Who the hell is this guy anyway? I never seem to be able to get it right. Oh, I've managed on the odd occasion, but generally it's a day of expectations, never quite lived up to.

Nevertheless this time round I think I do alright. Flowers and a card in the morning, a baby sitter (my mum) and a nice meal in the evening. With a five month old child at home that's about as good as it's going to get.

Unfortunately it comes just after our newly imposed Nanny McPhee routine has failed, and Erin is a little down about it to say the least. It *is* pretty depressing I must admit, to be seeing a bit of light at the end of the tunnel and then... gone. I wasn't living with it day in, day out though, and I'm able to see it in a more philosophical light perhaps.

Kids are just like that, good days and bad days, that's just the way it is and you have to get used it. I don't see any point in getting *too* depressed about it, not for too long anyway. This is just the start of parenthood. If we are constantly getting depressed about every single thing that doesn't go according to plan—then we really are going to be fucked.

Erin is right in the middle of it though and doesn't have the distance that I do. She is faced with a wee girl whom she is convinced has something wrong with her, but can't quite figure out what. Crying non-stop, no sleep, every single day.

As it turns out she was right of course, but we'll get to that later.

I try to express my concern over dinner, and once again ruin a perfectly decent Valentine's Day. I am getting worried about Erin though, about her seeming 'obsession' with Katie's sleep and I have to try, have to say something.

Maybe it doesn't come out so well, or maybe Erin has just had enough, but anyway, I am told in no uncertain terms that I don't know what it's like, and this is the hardest it's been since the little lady was born.

She is now so down that she is actually afraid to get her hopes up again, she tells me. I am genuinely worried about her, although it appears not to have come out the right way. Bloody Valentine's Day.

Anyway, despite us struggling through our sleep issues and having the odd argument (because we are exhausted basically) there is also an awful lot of good stuff going on right now.

As I said my mum has arrived, and once again it is great to 'show off' our beautiful wee girl.

The stories of me as a nightmare child are reinforced with more detail, and I can believe my mum when she tells me there was a constant twitch in her eye for a couple of years, thanks to me. Sounds like I am reaping what I sowed all these years before.

Katie starts to shimmy a wee bit on the ground, getting ready to crawl and it's all very exciting.

There is a funny wee incident too, once again related to sleep. You'll be aware by now that kids do not sleep like us, at all. The more tired you get as an adult, the quicker you'll be able to nod off when your head finally hits the pillow. It's the exact opposite for babies. If they don't get to sleep when they're supposed to, they start to get worked up, hyper, and getting them down to sleep becomes nigh on impossible.

Sure, on the odd occasion as a grown up you become overtired and can't get to sleep—but it doesn't make you go hyperactive and mental—like Katie is when Erin takes her along to a Baby CPR course one afternoon.

I wish I'd been there to see it. It's a group activity organised by the local midwife showing how to do CPR on an infant. All the mothers are given a little plastic baby to practice on, and while the other kids sit around nicely, Katie (who is overtired and going berserk by this time) decides to gnaw the face off Erin's dummy. It gets so bad that eventually they have to leave. All these nice little kids and their mothers, horrified by Hannibal Lector chowing down on her latest victim! Ha! I'd have loved to have been there!

Five months down, fun 'n games indeed.

How to get a baby to sleep: Facts of life

Babies are, surprise, surprise, all very different. There do seem to be categories of sensitivity however. Where your baby falls on this scale will have an enormous effect on your life—and your ability to keep them calm, and asleep. Instructions as follows, you'll be starting to notice a pattern here. Nothing's guaranteed, but start at the beginning and see how you go.

—Feed them
—Change their nappy
—Cuddle them
—Take them into a dark room and cuddle them—only for younger babies
—Tell them to go the fuck to sleep
—Wrap them up well (swaddle)

If none of the above works, then just keep trying. At three months, they're supposed to calm down a little bit, but if your kid isn't sleeping on a reasonably continuous basis soon after that, you'll need to get into some technique. Good luck, but if none of them work, there is a last bastion of hope for parents who are probably wishing they never had a kid in the first place—the Tresillian sleep clinic.

This is like boot camp for you and your baby. I've heard stories of it working, and stories of it *not* working. Just your luck. We didn't go, as we ended up hiring Nanny McPhee instead. I'm not convinced they would have been able to do anything anyway. Once again if you had the answer to this, you'd be rich enough to make even Solomon blush.

22

Six Months: Illness And Glycerin

"If you have never been hated by your child you have never been a parent."
— Bette Davis. **You said it lady.**

It shouldn't really be funny, but I can't help myself. Watching Katie's wee face and the colour she turns when she gets her immunisations. They come in the form of a twin set of jabs and there is such outrage in her expression, I just have to laugh.

It is a good way to do it actually, they have three nurses in there, one to hold her down and the other two dealing with a chubby little arm each. Having been there when a doctor cut the skin tags in her eyes, this is nothing.

She settles back down again quickly. I am surprised, although I'm sure there is a look in her eye when we leave the clinic. I am now a father not to be trusted…won't be the last time I get *that* look I'm sure.

We are told to expect a little bit of fever in response to the injections, and there's certainly no laughter on my part when she can't even hold her hands up to her bottle later on in the day. She just lies there shivering. Poor wee soul. We are up quite a few times through the night, and thank god for Panadol.

At least we knew what the cause was, and we manage the situation. About the crying and the sleeplessness however, we've received so many conflicting opinions as to what it might be. Nobody seems to know. I'm beginning to think that's just what babies are like, nothing you can do about it.

First of all our local doctor tells us it's reflux, and we should start her on Zantac straight away. Reflux is where the sphincter muscle at the top of your stomach isn't fully formed, and it's quite common in premature babies like Katie. Because the muscle can't close properly, acid from the stomach pops back up into the throat. It plays up more often in the afternoon too, which would be why Katie wasn't sleeping very well then. Zantac is a seriously strong medicine however, so we are loathe to give it to her unless she really needs it.

Then someone else says it's probably constipation that's causing it all—and we should hold off on the Zantac. Roll on another day or two and a naturopath we had been recommended says something different altogether.

It's amazing how many differing perspectives there seem to be, depending on which doctor you speak to.

It's not very comforting, and over time we eventually discover we just have to trust our own judgement, and have faith in our own instincts. Informed by what the various doctors are saying of course, but we make the decision as to *who* to listen to, and to what extent.

I had almost decided to ignore what the naturopath was saying for example, until she mentions that Katie is very young to be crawling as well as she is, and that this shows a great deal of intelligence. Oh well, now, here's a lady who knows what she's talking about!

The coordination required to get the arms and legs moving to crawl is apparently very advanced. Studies have shown that babies who crawl early do much better at school. The right and left sides of the brain have to be speaking to each other very efficiently for it to work, and many babies don't even crawl at all. Just shuffle about on their arses. I am so filled with pride when I hear this I could burst. Whether it's true or not, who knows—I don't care.

Enlightened naturopath aside, we eventually give Katie what I suspect is a rather unnatural remedy—a glycerin suppository. It does the trick for a day or two, then back to the same old situation. Hey ho.

Meanwhile Erin is just exhausted. She is also frustrated by the fact that she *knows* there is something wrong with Katie, but doesn't know what.

Meanwhile having my mum and Jim over here now is just great. Mum is truly in love with Katie, and having some help around the house makes a real difference for us too.

My mum is also with us when Katie, with her great intelligence of course, invents a completely new form of transport. The mud-skipper manoeuver. She shuffles with her arms a wee bit, arches her back, torso up straight, then launches her upper body forwards into a belly flop. It's hilarious. And not long after that she is crawling around everywhere, getting into everything, trying to eat plants, climbing up cushions to break out the barricades of her makeshift enclosures, even standing up straight when she does this.

Although I said I wasn't going to mention developmental stages very much, six months is a significant time for a child. It's when you're supposed to start giving them solid food, and for us, it truly is a turning point.

We start, and she just doesn't take to it. She refuses to eat, and it takes us an unbelievable amount of time just to coax her into a couple of mouthfuls. It is incredibly frustrating.

She is so small, and we know she needs to grow because the midwives and the doctors keep telling us she is too small for her age, but she's just not having it.

Nobody knew back then, but food was actually the main source of our problems.

23

Intermission

"That was the thing about the world: it wasn't that things were harder than you thought they were going to be, it was that they were hard in ways that you didn't expect."
—Lev Grossman. **Yes indeed.**

OK. Break. Of course in real life you can't do this. There's no pause button, no nicking out for popcorn and a visit to the toilet before returning to your life. Actually there used to be. Before your kid came along you could go away for a couple of days and relax, bugger off to the hills for a weekend or even a week if you needed. Not anymore.

So, six months into it, and looking back now was I right to be terrified of becoming a father and losing my freedom? Well, yes, I was. I can't just head off whenever I feel like it. I can't just go to the pub on a whim, go for lunch that ends up turning into dinner because we've been sitting at the table so long. And I certainly can't pack up a rucksack and buy a one-way ticket anymore.

On the other hand, as I've already said—I don't really *want* to go anywhere. Sure on the odd occasion (perhaps in the middle of a lengthy PUPD session) I'd happily disappear to Greece on my own, but overall I am very content, very happy.

And have my priorities changed? Was there anything wrong with them in the first place? Well, yes, they *have* changed, but no there was nothing wrong with my priorities back then either, just as there's nothing wrong with them now. It's just different. Different stages in life.

I remember reading an interview of Alan Arkin, who I last saw in the movie 'Argo' telling people to 'Argo fuck themselves' (which endeared him to me tremendously) and he was explaining how the only certainty in life now, was change. On a number of occasions he thought he'd figured it all out, then everything changed. This had happened so frequently he'd come to accept it as the only certainty—that's just the way life is.

Becoming a father, and having your priorities oriented towards your child and your family, is just a natural progression of life. It's a good thing, although a little trying, and tiring and all the rest of it, good nonetheless. Marriage, or living with someone for a long time is a small step towards it, but even still, it's a huge jump to go from partnered up to parenthood. Marriage is all about compromise, but it's easy still to be selfish, just a little bit. If you're lucky, you get your own way at least half of the time.

A kid is where nothing is about you anymore. Certainly at this point in time anyway, six months into the whole deal—but once again, not a problem, not a bother, quite happy with it all.

So having expected the worst and hoped for the best, and my initial fears proving unfounded, is there anything I hadn't expected, any hidden surprises? Well, yes, continuously. On a day—to—day basis I frequently find myself in situations that I never would have guessed at, like the time Katie threw up—directly into my mouth… hmm, a surprise for sure.

On a big picture scale though, something I hadn't foreseen was that as a consequence of our living situation, with me at work and Erin at home with a baby, we've turned into some kind of parody of an old 1950s TV show, but with iPhones and the internet.

And it brings to the fore unconscious preconceptions about gender roles. Before I probably would have considered myself quite forward thinking in this regard, but now I'm not so sure. 'Dad' goes to work, comes home and hugs his wife and daughter, has dinner, takes the bins out and eventually crashes in front of the TV with a beer in hand, albeit only for 15 minutes or so before heading to bed. Meanwhile 'Mum' spends the day looking after the baby, tidies up the house a bit and gets dinner ready for 'Dad's' return. It is a little more complicated than that of course, but the traditional roles are there, undeniably so.

I can see us turning into what I suppose my mum and dad were—a traditional married couple with a family. I certainly didn't expect that. I don't think I'd ever thought that far ahead really, but here we are, and the main surprise is that I actually find it quite comforting. There's a nice feeling to providing for your family.

Another entirely different surprise of parenthood, which isn't comforting in the least, I might add, is the uncertainty around Katie's crying, sleeping and eating situation. I wasn't expecting there *not* to be answers to these things, and the fact that nobody knows what is going on leads to a difference of opinion between Erin and I.

In all the years we've been together, this has just never happened. We are both generally of a similar mind, on most things that count anyway. Now, we seem to be heading in different directions a little over Katie.

The sleep deprivation, the crying and all the rest of it was hard enough but manageable if we were together on it. This growing divergence however, was a worry all of its own—and as difficult as I thought it had been up to now, in the coming months it was about to get a whole lot harder.

24

Seven Months: Round The World And Back

"When my kids become wild and unruly, I use a nice, safe playpen. When they're finished, I climb out."
— Erma Bombeck. **Ha!**

A few words of advice to anyone thinking about traveling to the other side of the world with an infant, actually just one word of advice—don't.

So here's the trip. Leave Sydney and fly to Abu Dhabi for a four-day stopover. Catch up with a couple of friends, then on to Dublin. Picked up at the airport and driven to the Irish countryside, Erin's home—Ballyfin. Couple of days there, then back to Dublin (a nice seaside suburb called Malahide) where we stay for another four days and Katie is christened.

After the christening, I drive back to Glasgow with my mum and Jim, over on the ferry from Belfast and I have five days in Glasgow before Erin and Katie arrive. In the meantime, they move out of the hotel in Malahide, and in with Deirdre and Martin (Erin's sister and brother in law) and their kids.

Saturday morning they arrive in Glasgow, and that afternoon we have my family round to say hi. Sunday afternoon all my old school friends descend with their kids—about 40 people in total. Good fun, but not very relaxing.

Monday to Friday, we try to chill but there doesn't seem to be time, a little, but not enough. The following Saturday Erin, Katie and I fly to Dublin. We're picked up and out to Ballyfin again. The next day I'm picked up by my friend Pete (who's driven up from Cork) and he takes me up to Dublin. We go out for a bevy, I'm up at 6am the next morning, Deirdre takes me to the airport and I'm offski back to Sydney. Erin and Katie stay in Ballyfin before flying back three weeks later.

Phew… I'm exhausted just thinking about it, and that's before you throw in the fact that Katie hardly slept at all for the whole freakin' trip, and she picked up a cold in Ireland that took about four months to shift. Pffft.

The problem wasn't actually going to the other side of the world, it was the amount of moving around we did when we got there. I don't think holidays are ever going to be the same again. I would strongly advise go somewhere, stay in the same place for the whole time, then come home again.

Any sleep pattern you might have established goes out the window. Well it did with Katie anyway. And although we were with family over there, at three in the morning there's nobody but you and your partner on duty.

I came home after all of this feeling more knackered than I was at the start, and that's saying something. Still, it was worse for Erin because when I was gone, she was the only one there for the late night parenting, and it was hard work.

That's the overview. However, let's go back to the start and fill in the details. Let's get into 'packing' to go to the other side of the world with an infant. Considering it takes about an hour to get ready to leave the house for a coffee, can you imagine how long the process takes..?

Well… two weeks. It takes about two weeks, of planning, making lists—and then the actual packing itself. New bags are purchased, the whole thing is meticulous. Nothing to do with me at all, as you might have guessed.

Faced with the prospect of keeping Katie entertained for 30 hours or so, we throw in everything we can think of. So packed, ready, and optimistic—we head off to the airport. It's a late flight and we hope that Katie will sleep soon after we're seated. Unfortunately however, it is a wee bit *too* late. Just beyond the sleep window so Katie's temperament, and hence ours, is in the hands of the gods.

We manage fine to begin with. Check in, a bite to eat, a couple of visits to the 'Parents' Rooms' in the airport— and eventually we board the airplane. It is quite exciting really, here we are heading back home, after years on the other side of the world—and we are bringing our beautiful wee daughter home with us… 'Look what we've done! Isn't she great?!'

Half an hour into the flight things are going reasonably well—apart from the constant squirming, which quite frankly we are expecting. Overall not as horrific as you might have feared. Then Murphy's Law kicks in. Katie squirms a little more vehemently, a bottle of water pours into my lap and she starts to cry. 'Ah, here we go'. I am now one of the people I used to try and avoid. The ones with a screaming kid on a plane.

A wee hint for you if you ever take a little one on an airplane. Think twice before booking the 'bulkhead' seat. We opted for that, and bugger me what a pain in the ass. It sounds like a good idea. They don't get a seat until they're two but with the bulkhead, there's a wee basket where they can sleep. You don't have them sitting in your lap, or squashed in between you all the time.

However, picture the scene. You've managed to mop up your crotch, and your trousers don't feel *too* wet anymore. Your underwear is another story. However you've managed to get a couple of hours into the flight and you're still alive. Happy days. Your kid has played with her toys, drunk her milk, she's gone through her hyperactive stage—and eventually passed out from sheer exhaustion. You've managed to manhandle the little blighter into the portacot, which is the only reason you're sitting there, and finally—you're rewarded with a moment of peace. Ahh. Flip up the movie console maybe? What's on? Nothing you've seen because going to the movies isn't something you do anymore. Hmmm. Select some action nonsense that takes very little thought, and breathe. Then the plane enters a little patch of turbulence and your baby begins to stir—but a comforting hand settles her down, and if you have to sit with a hand on the little one for a while, so be it.

This is when some bitch of an air stewardess comes by and tells you that you have to take your fucking baby out of the portacot. 'Ah, well thanks for your advice dear, but I don't think you realise, my daughter's actually asleep? And if I take her out, that'll wake her up. Ahh, you do realise that. Hmm. You don't care? What the fuck?! Are you fucking kidding me?!' But alas, no, they are not kidding. You have to take your kid out the bloody portacot—every time there's a little bit of turbulence. Even though there's a seat belt over them while they're in there. That was it for us, we didn't put her back in for the whole flight. What a fucking waste of time.

Katie is as good as a hyperactive little kid *can* be on a trip to the other side of the world. Erin and I take turns walking her up and down the plane, as she only sits in your arms for so long before squirming. She wants to move, to shuffle, to climb, she wants to do anything but sit there with us holding her.

One row in front, and to the side across the aisle, a lovely Lebanese woman takes Katie off our hands for a wee while. She is one of the ones who look on with a smile, a knowing glance and an ounce of pity. She's been there. She knows what it is like. She is taking her teenage daughter back to Lebanon to visit her homeland—and she knows what we are going through. People you meet like that are absolute gems. Most just ignore you, or even worse, give you that disapproving glare. Like you're a bad fucking parent if you can't control these little balls of flesh, muscle and instinct.

Anyway, god bless her, she gives us about 20 minutes of peace, lovely. It's amazing how much a little gesture, a little effort, can make a disproportionately large impact on people's lives, at least for a day, or a few moments.

A long haul flight with an infant: Facts of life
Think twice before you take the bulkhead seat, as your kid will be evicted from the portacot at the first sign of turbulence. Take everything you can possibly imagine. You never know what's going to keep them interested. Take some new toys they've never seen before. If they like watching a bit of telly now and again—deprive them of it for two weeks or so before you fly. Take all sorts of food, drinks, anything that will keep them occupied.

Try to have them sucking on a bottle during the actual take—off, as the swallowing action helps prevent their ears getting blocked with the pressure. Same when you're coming down to land. Take lots of spare clothes for them, and a few items for yourself. Make sure you're well fed before you get on the plane too, because it's entirely possible you might not get anything to eat. If lunch or dinner comes by and you have a sleeping kid on your lap, tough. Some of them will bring you food later, some won't.

No matter how many toys and distractions you bring however, eventually your kid is going to get pissed off with the whole situation. You just have to deal with it—as does anyone else sitting nearby.

Katie didn't really freak out too much, there was a lot of moving around, a bit of narkiness—but overall she did great. There were other kids nearby who cried the house down. It didn't upset me though, I just felt sorry for them.

So we survive our first long haul flight, and arrive in Abu Dhabi. Our 'not even one year old' is now an international traveler. We're booked into a Sheraton hotel with a couple of pools. This is going to be the only 'holiday' part of the whole holiday, so we want to make it as comfortable as possible.

The stop off serves two purposes. One, to break the journey and two, to catch up with a couple of friends who live in the Middle East. Tanya and Alan. First of all, let me quickly tell you how I met Tanya. It's one of those 'small world' stories.

I was at Glasgow University at the time, and I was sitting in the queue of the student travel agency. I was there for quite a while I might add, so I struck up a conversation with a Canadian girl next to me. I knew she was Canadian because she had a back pack with the maple leaf sewn onto it of course. You know, the way they all do—in case someone mistakes them for an American. Having been mistaken for an Englishman previously, I understand.

Anyway, she was visiting her Glaswegian granny for a few days before heading off to Greece to work on an archaeological dig, and I gallantly offered to show her a bit of the Scottish countryside before she left. What a gent. It was a bit of a risk I guess, for a single girl to take off to the hills in a car with a total stranger, but, as Tanya laughingly says now "He was kinda small, so I figured I could take him if there were any hassles". Very funny. Anyway, off we went to Loch Lomond, and low and behold my car breaks down. We had to go knocking on the door of this little old lady's house, and fortunately she was delightful. Fed us cups of tea and scones like we were long lost relatives until my mum could come out and tow us back to the city. Gallant indeed.

Tanya's granny was none too impressed about the time I got her back to the house that evening, and to this day, Granny Kane still thinks I'm 'bad news'.

We kept in touch the only way you could back then, by letter, and a couple of months later I received a note from Greece, telling me what Tanya's father had said about our encounter. As is turns out, he used to work for my dad in his fledgling design agency, before moving to Canada, and here we were bumping into each other randomly in a travel agent's queue, 20 years later.

We both knew that it was far too much of a coincidence not to keep in touch, and we're great friends to this day. Tanya even came to live in Glasgow for a while, and that's where she met a hilarious English teacher, now lawyer, now husband, and soon to be father of twins, Alan. They live in Oman, and are flying over to spend a couple of days with us in Abu Dhabi.

This is Tanya's first time having kids too, and we are able to give her a full run down. It is nice to be able to do that, to talk it all through with a good friend, especially having been in the exact same situation ourselves, only a few months ago. She has all the same questions, and the same concerns that Erin and I experienced during the pregnancy. We try, as much as possible, to allay those fears. I'm not entirely sure how effectively but hey—we hadn't had twins—that will be a different ball game altogether.

We lap up the luxury for a couple of days, but most of the time we are both so exhausted, we can't properly appreciate it. The best part of it all is playing in the pool with Katie. She just loves it, and whenever she is awake we try to bring her down to the kids' pool for a crawl around.

Another piece of advice for you here: if you're planning on staying in a hotel room with a baby, you need to know things you would have never even considered before.

For example, our plan was to put the portacot into the bathroom during the day, so that we could lie on our five star luxury bed for a couple of hours watching cable TV movies. A rare treat. However, we hadn't banked on that fact that the TV audio was piped into the bathroom, and couldn't be switched off. So our planned indulgence was scuppered.

Hardly the end of the world, but an indication of the level of detail you need to go into if you want to make a couple of days in a hotel as comfortable as possible.

Truth be told, we've still not managed to crack this type of thing yet. And, in fact, for years we avoided taking Katie anywhere unless we had to—as her already bad sleeping habits were even worse if she wasn't at home.

Nevertheless, this was the most relaxing part of the entire journey. Next step—a nine hour flight to Ireland, and the big reception committee.

Did I mention the level of noise that can be produced by just a couple of members of Erin's family? I think I did. So when we finally make it back to the farm, and into the dining room by the kitchen (where absolutely everything goes on) the decibels reach hitherto unheard-of levels. I'm terrified, Erin is home, and happy, and Katie—who has half of those genes after all—is loving it.

Despite the noise, the jet lag and the total lack of sleep in general, I must admit it is exciting to be here and for everyone to meet little Katie. And for Erin, it's a wonderful moment.

For the next few days Katie is the absolute centre of attention, her favourite place to be—and we get busy settling her into the new environment. Babies, you'll realise eventually yourself, are easier to deal with when you're at home. You have the room set up right, you know where everything is, you have a 'place' for the bottles, the nappies, the wipes, and all the paraphernalia that goes along with it.

Move out of your safety zone, and you've generally got a bit of fixin' to do. The room has a skylight, for example, but no blind to cover it. So we have to fiddle about with a ladder and put some tinfoil up to keep the light out. The cot is new for the little lady, she isn't particularly keen on it, and we have the new time zone to deal with of course too.

All of this is no big deal really. The worst part about not being at home, is being in someone else's home. The rhythms of the house are not those of an infant's, and when your little one is up all night crying, you know you're waking an entire household.

With family it's bearable of course—they have no choice, but staying in a friend's house would be trying for everyone involved.

Anyway, just as we seem to be getting there, it is time to pack up and move again—to another hotel room, another environment and another cot. The Grand Hotel in Malahide for the christening. See what I mean about moving around too much? Give it a miss if you possibly can. Anyway, this is a wonderful part of the holiday. A real celebration. Bringing both families together, friends too—and I enjoy it immensely. Katie plays her part well during the service, and we all manage to get a few drinks in over a couple of days. The hotel even has a babysitter, who looks after her one night while we all have a bite to eat in the hotel restaurant. Another service to look out for if you're booking a hotel.

Next, I'm off back to Scotland, and Erin and Katie move into her sister's house in Malahide for a couple of days. Another household kept up all night—but not one that I'm in, for the first time in what seems like forever.

Nostalgia trip

My mum and Jim drove over from Scotland for the Christening, and I join them for the trip home. North from Dublin, into Northern Ireland and onto Belfast. From there, over on the ferry to Stranraer, and an hour or so along the coast back to Glasgow.

It's a lovely wee trip. A nice way to go home. Slowly, on a boat, and I savour the journey, the time, the release of responsibility and the ability to finish a thought without interruption. It's freezing outside on the deck of the ferry. I'm the only one out here, and I'm loving it. Every black wave, every dark cloud, and eventually, every rain drop. Loving my slow, trip, home.

We've been in Australia for seven years, and it's five since I visited Scotland. I'm looking forward to seeing the hills again, walking the streets of Glasgow and catching up with old friends.

Glasgow is a great city. Big enough to have everything you could possibly want, but not quite big enough to overwhelm you or make you feel insignificant. And, having lived there for 30 years or so—there is hardly a corner of it I'm not acquainted with. Memories at every turn, and I'm looking forward to seeing how the 'ol place is bearing up.

I have a few days on my own before Erin and Katie arrive, and there is a list of things I want to do. On the other hand, I also want to do nothing. I manage a hike up the hills, a proper bevy one night, one of my good mates finally comes out of the closet, I visit old haunts and I walk the streets for a while. And, to top it all off, I manage a day lying on the couch watching TV—with my mum shuttling me the odd bite to eat now and again. Utter bliss. Altogether it's a perfect little taste of Scotland.

No matter how long I live anywhere else, I'll always be a Glaswegian. There's something about Glasgow that just stays with you. An attitude. A way of looking at the world. A no—bullshit, struggling to be optimistic, yet extremely funny approach to life and everything it throws at you.

That's actually one of the things that I feel conflicted about — that it looks as if my daughter will be growing up on the other side of the world. Growing up without that Glaswegian attitude, and the humour that goes with it, embedded in her psyche. But I guess that's my job as her father—to instill that in her.

Everyone who moves away from their homeland must feel that potential for loss.

It's almost like a mild guilt, as if you're doing something illicit and hoping nobody finds out. Like you're cheating on your own country.

I read somewhere about people who live abroad, saying that they end up being from nowhere. In their new country they're always a bit of an outsider, and when they go back to their own country, they find that they've changed so much they don't really fit in anymore. They've ruined it for themselves.

I don't buy into that. Although it took a long time to get here, I feel quite at home in Australia now, and I always feel at home in Scotland. I didn't leave Glasgow because I didn't like it. It was just that I wanted to see more. To broaden my horizons and go exploring. Although it's a great place, Glasgow (like most places I'm sure) can be quite insular sometimes—and it was this that I had no interest in.

Funny though, seven years on I could do with a bit of insularity. I could do with a bit of comfort, the kind that comes from familiarity. Many of my friends had kids way before I left home—and I'm looking forward to catching up with them all over the coming days, now I'm a parent too.

In a way, I kind of miss the fact that I'm going through this wonder of my child growing up, without the comfort of the friends I grew up with myself.

Further into it all now however, I'm meeting lots of new and interesting people over here in Sydney. Katie's friends' parents, and many of them are in the same boat as us. Living abroad with very little family support.

The other bonus is that I'll be able to provide Katie with the best of what both countries have to offer, never mind Ireland too. If Erin and I can bring all three countries to bear in Katie's upbringing, what a lucky kid.

Anyway, my dose of familiarity starts the afternoon Erin and Katie arrive in Glasgow and my mum's side of the family come round to say hi. It is lovely to see them. It's amazing, actually, what a little baby can do to a family. Our lot weren't quite as noisy as Erin's (that would be a physical impossibility) but the oohs and ahs are impossible to contain.

My mum's sister, May, and my cousins Mark and Kim were a big part of my childhood. Every weekend for years, we would all visit my Gran and Grandpa together. Mark and Kim were also instructed on how to catch a scorpion with a shoelace, how to make a tank out of a cigarette packet. Mark and I would fight behind the couches, tearing lumps out of each other as cups of tea and sandwiches were consumed round a couple of red bars on the electric fire. Mark had learned Judo however, and he also had a few years on me, so I wasn't that bothered to be on the receiving end of a half pretzel now and again. He learned with his dad, my Uncle

Andy who was, and still is, hilarious. I always thought he was a pretty cool dad, and there was always laughter round their house.

One time I'll never forget. I was playing football in the garden with Mark. Andy was there too, as was a big black Labrador they had at the time. I can't remember his name, but he was a big fella of that I can assure you, because before too long I tripped, and landed head first in one of his enormous shites. Right on my forehead. And in my hair. Aaarghh. To this day, I can remember it vividly.

Aunty May managed to hold in her laughter, probably so she didn't have to breathe too much, as she kindly stuck my head in the kitchen sink and scrubbed away until it all came out.

Mark, Kim and Andy on the other hand couldn't contain themselves. If it hadn't been *my* head landing in the massive dog shit I'd have been rolling about in fits too. As I said, always laughter round their house.

Character building I guess. Life, as they say, etching itself into my soul. Why is it that character building is always so bloody awful at the time though?

Anyway, as we sit in the living room now with cups of tea and biscuits, I look at Kim's kids and can't help thinking 'How did that happen so quickly?' We're the oldies now.

My nostalgia trip continues when all my old school friends come round to catch up at Jim's house the next day. Fortunately the weather is beautiful, so we have a barbeque outside. Loads of kids running around, and a garden full of old friends who don't see that much of each other anymore. Great.

I'd really been looking forward to seeing everyone, and as we talk, I discover that everybody seems to have had a distinctly different experience of parenthood so far. Some easier than others, some chaotic, and one friend in particular had some reasonably serious issues to deal with. I feel for them, and it makes me feel better about what we are going through. It is nice chatting about it all. Talking to people I know so well, I can ask anything at all, without worry or cause for concern.

Did they find it as hard as we seem to be? Did they sleep? How old were their kids when they slept through the night? When did it all get a bit easier? Did they want to shoot themselves in the head on the odd occasion?

Everyone has a different answer, which is nice to hear actually. Changed days. Happy days though.

Family, friends, and a treat of a day to ourselves, then we're off back to Dublin, and back to Ballyfin. More moving around for Katie, and her sleep is even worse than usual. Erin and I both feel as if we've been hit by a bus. A big one too, one of those articulated mother fuckers. At least we don't have to go to work though. And the London Olympics are on right now, so when we are trying to catch up on our sleep at all times during the day, we can watch a bit of sporting history before we get our heads down. Mo Farra and Super Saturday. Awesome.

Time to leave my family

After another couple of frantic days around the farm in Ballyfin, it's time for me to leave. Just me this time. Not me and my family. Erin's mum drives Erin, Katie and me to the outskirts of Dublin where we meet up with my good friend Pete—one of the Kiwis I met years before playing rugby in Colorado.

It's a little unsettling, leaving Erin and Katie. I'm not going to see them for three weeks, but I have to swallow my tears as I jump into the passenger seat next to an old buddy. I haven't seen Pete in a long, long time, and crying like a baby would *not* be the best way to pick up the friendship.

Pete's a lovely guy, and not unlike most Kiwis, a bit of a traveler himself.

After a degree in business studies and a couple of years' working, he decided it was time to venture a little further. His journey took him round America playing rugby first of all, and that's where we met. We both played on the same team at Boulder Rugby Club.

I remember meeting him for the first time in Aspen, where we were playing in a tournament. Then the next day, after an almighty piss up in the winter playground of America's wealthiest folks, I saw him wandering around on his own, just toddling down the street. Turns out his lift had gone and he was trying to figure out what his next move would be. There was room in the car I was taking back to Boulder, so we gave him a lift, and we've been friends ever since.

Pete was one of the 'funny talkers' I ended up living with, in an apartment in (and I can't believe I remember this) Colgate Street, in Boulder. Actually, it was more of a basement, but we made it pretty comfortable. We built a bar, and… ah, actually that's about all we did. We threw a few mattresses on the ground, and a couch in one of the rooms. That was all the comfy we needed. Ahh, those were the days.

Unbelievable how Pete could have torn himself away from such salubrious surroundings. However, he left to play rugby somewhere else in the states before eventually heading overseas to Ireland. And it was there that he, like I, had fallen for an Irish lass.

His intention had been to have a few years abroad, then return to New Zealand where he'd been accepted into medical school. Life, however, had other plans—and here we are 20 years later…

Pete is married with two kids, and medical school is a distant memory. I'd kept in touch since Boulder, so I knew that Pete and Fiona had been through some tough times. They'd been through years of IVF, and it had put them through the wringer. But they'd made it, and here they were with two lovely wee kids, and life was good.

I think he would have happily moved back to New Zealand, but it was not to be, and he had accepted that his life was in Ireland for the foreseeable future. Not a bad place at all.

Once again, it is nice to really talk through this kind of stuff with someone I know so well. Someone who, like me, enjoys traveling and exploring different places. Again it is comforting to see a friend who has an adventurous spirit, living his life very happily with two kids in tow.

That night, possibly for the first time ever for the two of us, we leave the pub before closing time. I have to get up early for my flight back, and I want to be able to enjoy the luxury of flying alone without a baby, without a hangover. So we pull the plug before we get too drunk. We even eat half way through the night. For a couple of old rugby mates this is sensible stuff indeed.

And that was the end of my trip. A three week whirlwind. I manage to wake up the next day feeling not too bad, then fly half way round the world to an empty home. All I have to do now, is move house.

25

Eight Months: Separation Anxiety

"Humans are the only animals who have children on purpose, with the exception of guppies, who like to eat theirs."
—P.J. O'Rourke. **That's an idea…**

I watch a couple of movies on the flight home and then sleep like the dead, or like a guy who's just had a holiday with an infant. People who say 'slept like a baby' have obviously never had a baby, or they've had a really 'good' one who sleeps all the time. Either way, right now if someone tells me to 'sleep like a baby' I'd probably knock the motherfucker out.

Anyway the trip home, and the peace and quiet is bliss. As soon as I get home however, it's all go.

✯ ✯ ✯

The removal man says it's probably the worst packing job he's ever seen. I'm not sure what customer service book he's been reading, but insulting your client just as you're about to do some work for them is not exactly the best way to start a relationship.

If I wasn't in a bind, I'd tell him to fuck off right now. I think the world would be a better place if we all had a bit more fuck off inside of us actually. But alas, sometimes we just need things to be done.

Apart from the fractured start however, the move goes fine. The idiot of a removal man receives zip for a tip, and I'm left with the usual cardboard box chaos to get stuck into. It takes a while.

Getting the house ready for a baby
As you can imagine, there are lots of things you *can* do, but not so many you actually have to do. I had a look online before writing this, and I couldn't believe some of the crap that people out there were saying. I guess it depends on how much time you have on your hands, and, once again—how much you do just to get into the spirit of it all before the little one arrives.

For example, one site says that you should buy little 'power plug' covers, so your kid doesn't electrocute himself. Now I'm all for that, non-electrocution is a fantastic way to bring up your child, but, considering your newborn isn't able to move very much for a year or so—unless you lay them next to a power point, stick a screw driver in their hand and direct it into the socket, you're not going to have any problems. Best to spend your time before the little one arrives *not* doing shit like that. Rather, going to a movie in the afternoon, going for a hike, reading an entire book in one day or drinking three bottles of wine for lunch.

Realistically though, to begin with all you really need is a place to keep the stuff, the wipes, the nappies, the powders. If you have a spare room, perfect, that's your nursery. If not, put it all where it's going to be most accessible.

It also depends on where the little one is going to be sleeping for the first wee while. If they'll be sleeping in your room, they'll be in a little cot called a basinet.

We kept Katie in with us for about six months, and, because the basinet was so light, I could actually pick it up while she was asleep and put her outside the door for a while. This allowed us not to be constantly on edge with her breathing and pretending to be dead tactics. So we had some of the bits and pieces in our room, but most of it stored in her nursery. Whatever room they'll be sleeping in, you do need to ensure you can get the room properly dark, and can manage the temperature.

It's all about enabling them to sleep as easily as possible. You do *not* want to do anything that will impair sleep. And that's all you need to worry about, all you *really* need to prepare before a baby arrives. Further down the line, you can have a go at the plug covers, the plastic corners, the drawer closers, and make sure there are no cords hanging down from blinds or curtains.

By the time the move is completed and I've unpacked, it feels as if I've been going for about a year—which is about right. Although I manage to catch up on my sleep, there isn't much time for R&R. I'm not even interested in going for a bevvy with my mates. Catching up on sleep is the number one priority.

It takes me about a week to get over a night out nowadays, and time is too precious for that. I'm too freakin' busy anyway! Come to think of it, I don't know what I used to do with all the time I had before Katie came along. When I think back to the days before she arrived… why didn't I get so much more done? I've had a hankering to learn the guitar for ages, but never done anything about it… Why the hell not!? What was I doing?

I call Erin every night and hear what they've been up to. Katie is in her element on the farm, running around with her little cousins and her Uncle John on his tractor. She helps

Nana feed the cats every morning out the back door, and helps Papa with the dog. She has lots of chores every day and is having a ball– despite the fact that her cold has refused to move, and her sleep is even worse than usual. Erin is enjoying being around her family too. They're a very close bunch and the only problem is, once again, severe lack of sleep, a killer.

I'm finding it hard back in Sydney on my own too, although I'm sure Erin would laugh at me for saying that. I had thought that I might enjoy a bit of time to myself, but it isn't quite what I was expecting.

After a day at work is over I usually have a bit of 'moving house' stuff to do, then something to eat—a phone call to Erin, then off to bed. I am missing them dreadfully. I joke, to any poor sod who will listen, that they have 'ruined my life'. Not only am I bloody knackered and dying for some time on my own when I'm with them, but when I finally have some time to myself, I can't enjoy it because I miss them so much! Aaaaargh!

Erin's family is a busy one, in that, there's always something going on round the farm, always something to do—and our phone calls are not as regular as I would like them to be. I am hanging out for these calls. Even though we might not have a lot to talk about it is important for me to stay connected with them. I can feel the connection kind of slipping a wee bit though. And it's horrible.

I write this in my phone at the airport, picking them up.

'Waiting for them to come through customs, very much looking forward to seeing them. Feel actually a little nervous, hope Katie remembers who I am… People filtering through now…. Also pretty tired, been a tough time at work lately. Feels like ages since I've seen them. Was a bit funny on the phone sometimes to begin with. Erin and Katie were having a bad time, and I was exhausted with the trip and the move, but we got over that. They were supposed to be coming home tomorrow morning, so when the call came last night saying it was tonight it was a bit of a surprise! Was going to be finishing off and cleaning the house tonight! Just bought a Nemo balloon, getting even more excited as more people are coming through.'

And here they are…

26

Nine Months: I'm On The Outside

"Families are about love overcoming emotional torture."
— Matt Groening. **No comment…**

I don't know if being apart for three weeks was a terribly good idea. Erin and Katie seem to have their own way of doing things now, and it doesn't include me. Katie won't let me put her down to sleep anymore, won't let me spend much time with her at all before whining for her mummy.

All the little tasks and rituals of living with an infant have changed too, and I have to learn them all over again. It also seems that when I do something wrong (or not the way they've been doing it in Ireland) I'm looked upon almost with ill-regard. In fact, I'm finding it hard to do anything right just now, and I feel like an outsider in my own family. It's frightening, and not a situation I ever expected to end up in, but then again, who does? I even find myself going to work and thinking on the way home, 'Nobody in there seems to like me. Where's the joy gone? Is this life? Is this it?'

From slightly different opinions over what might be wrong with Katie, or whether there even *was* anything wrong with her, to this? What the fuck?

With the benefit of hindsight, this is what I think happened.

We were having a tough time with Katie. Lack of sleep was killing us and we had virtually no support over here in Sydney—nobody to take Katie off our hands, even for an hour. Nobody to talk to about what we were doing with the little one, so were doing the best we could on our own. Reading books for guidance, whilst every single 'professional' we saw about Katie's sleeping and crying had a different opinion. We were barely keeping our heads above water.

Then Erin spent almost six weeks in the house she grew up in. Staying with her mum and dad who had raised six children, and living next door was her older brother John who had two kids of a similar age to Katie. It was a nurturing and caring environment, with hands on help and 'been there, done that' experience at every turn. When Erin came back to Oz it was just me, and I was out of the loop.

She was homesick, and I think because I felt like an outsider, I maybe acted a bit like that too—which made Erin pine for the security of her home back in Ireland even more. Hindsight. Instead of accepting that I was the outsider, and maybe, going in the huff about it, I should have been more forceful in pushing my way back in. I should have refused to accept the situation, because the way that I acted probably just fed the homesick fever even more.

Forget the sleep, forget the loss of freedom and all the other nonsense, this was without a doubt, the most difficult part of it all. This was the bit that justified the fear of becoming a father. The fact that two people who loved each other so much could retire to opposite corners of the earth, and return prepared for an emotional fight to the death. Such were the stresses, strains and worries of a sick child, no sleep and an unknown diagnosis. I couldn't imagine what years of this would do to a person.

It took us a while to get out of this spiral of negativity we seemed to have stumbled into, and truth be told I don't think there really was a Eureka moment when we popped out the other side. We just struggled through, and bit-by-bit we made it, thank god. Bringing up a kid is hard enough when you're both on the same team, but when the battle lines are drawn— it just eats away at your soul.

If you find yourself going through this at all, where you can't seem to put a foot right, where you seem to be arguing over how hot the milk is, or where you left your fuckin' shoes… don't worry, hang in there—and if you love each other you'll make it through. And it will make you stronger. I promise. Because nobody is enjoying that state of affairs. I think having been through it ourselves we'll both be incredibly careful never to let it get like that again.

Anyhow, meanwhile there's a wee lady who's not well, and still needs looked after whether her parents are utterly exhausted and in a huff with each other or not. And work is particularly busy right now too. Coffee consumption? Probably up to about 10 a day, although I wouldn't be surprised if it was more than that. I don't keep count, don't want to.

Childcare disasters

Then, after she's been 'without cold' for about a week, it is time for Katie to go to childcare for the first time. Unbelievable how quickly that's happened. I can remember going to check out some of the local childcare centres, and thinking how awful it would be to drop her off anywhere for the day. Nothing wrong with the centres, just that she's my little girl and she should be with her mummy and daddy.

Well, that's what I thought way back then, now we're a bit further down the line—I'm not quite as bothered about the prospect of her going somewhere for a day or two. I think Erin really needs the break, and I think getting back into work is going to be good for her too. Just to have something else to focus on apart from Katie, and to have that normal grown-up interaction again. All of that is going to help (as is the money!) and however hard it's going to be for the little lady, I'm sure she'll get used to it.

Unfortunately, it doesn't go well. In fact the word they use to describe Katie's second day at childcare (which is only three and a half hours) is 'disastrous'.

Erin drops her off for a couple of hours the first day, and when she comes back Katie has cried for almost the whole time. The second 'disastrous' day there is nothing *almost* about it, she cried non-stop for three and a half hours, no food, no sleep, nothing but tears and wailing. Oh, to be in childcare. No wonder it's so expensive.

After that episode the two of them have an appointment to see another practitioner we had been recommended, a homeopath this time I think. I speak to Erin after the appointment and I feel another one of those overwhelming urges to be with them.

Erin sounds so down, and Katie has had such a bad day. Suddenly there is nothing more important in the world than to be there, to help them out, look after them.

The last time that happened was when Erin told me we had three days, not three weeks, until Katie was going to be born. It was the same, almost primal reaction. That compulsion to act, accompanied by absolute certainty that I'm doing the right thing. I'm sure it is instinct actually, that deep down drive to protect your family. What could be more important? I make my excuses and leave. And when I get back home, it turns out that they are fine! So much for primal instinct.

The homeopath had another theory about what is wrong with Katie. She is just out of sorts because of the move to Ireland and back, moving house and having a cold for two months. No shit mate, thanks, how much was that?

Anyway, Erin, Katie and I begin to build our bridges. I spend a lot of time with Katie on my own at the weekends, giving Erin a break and allowing the little lady and I to get a bit of our connection back again. It's nice to be back in the fold.

27

Ten Months: Through The Wars

"Happiness is having a large, loving caring, close-knit family in another city."
—George Burns. **Hmm, not always.**

Finally getting comfortable in the new apartment helps too. The less chaos the better, and having moved from a three into a two bedroom place, we sell some bits and pieces, and buy a new dining table that doesn't take up half the house.

And once we're settled in, Katie starts to settle on her own two feet. Very exciting.

So kids don't just get up and take a few steps one day. Until I had one myself I probably would have thought that they did, but no. Katie stands for a couple of seconds at first, then longer, then for 10 seconds one day, then she tries to take a step and falls. She is getting there. It is close.

I can't wait, even though I've been told that when they start walking it's a real game changer. Hey ho, I am excited for her, you can see in her wee face that she is so pleased with herself when she stands for a while. It is great to watch.

Despite the fact that this is quite a notable event in a kid's life, the most memorable part of that tenth month for me was the illness, and in particular—the crack den.

Katie has started to get really ill, pretty much all the time. Childcare isn't working out and she hasn't done a full week (Tuesday, Thursday, Friday) since the beginning. We are called to pick her up virtually every other day, either because she won't stop crying, or because she has come down with something and her temperature has spiked dangerously high.

It is always something different she is catching, and always accompanied by a temperature of over 40 degrees, which is pretty unusual. Not completely unheard of, but for it to be happening this much is certainly not normal.

I didn't know this before but a high temperature is one of the ways that the body fights off infection. It's trying to make the environment inhospitable for whatever foreign body has invaded, and whether it's viral or bacterial, they are usually quite temperature sensitive. Once the heat is on, the rest of the immune system goes to work and tries to destroy the infection. So while a fever can be uncomfortable for a while, you should allow the body to do its thing, as the high temperature creates an environment that gives your immune system a better chance of fighting off the infection.

It's like rugby teams coming to Scotland, you're kind of hoping it rains—because in Scotland we know how to play in the rain better than everyone else in the world. Home advantage.

With an infant though, you need to be extremely careful how far you let that advantage extend. They tend to throw up when they get too hot, might become listless (believe me you'll know it when you see it) and because they're so lethargic you might find it difficult to get them to drink anything (to replace the fluids they lose when throwing up all the time).

If you're in this position and you can't bring the temperature down with Panadol, or Nurofen (we found

Nurofen to be longer lasting) then you need to go straight to hospital. Children can die from dehydration in these circumstances and in hospital they can put them on a drip, rehydrate, and also investigate properly to discover what is causing it all.

By now we are pretty adept at using a Nurofen and Panadol alternating system. And we are very strict with it, keeping a note of times, temperatures and doses—so we don't accidentally give her too much. The books say you should only use one of these at a time, but if you talk to your doctor, figure out how to handle it and what your little person can deal with, then you can use both on an alternating basis— and we need everything we can get our hands on right now.

Excerpt from Katie's illness book

Tuesday 29th June
    1am-34.9
    1:30am-35.6
    6am-40.2-2mls Nurofen
    1:30pm-40.5-1ml Nurofen
    6pm-35.8
    8:30pm-39.2
    10:26pm-39.3-2mls Nurofen

We're getting familiar with the healthcare system again, and one week I think we even have four trips to Sydney Children's Hospital. On this particular occasion it turns out she has bronchiolitis, which is a viral infection in the lungs. They put her on a drip and they want us to stay overnight, but they don't have any beds to admit us. We are happy to go back home anyway, get her into her room where she is more comfortable and keep an eye on her there. We're at the hospital so frequently now she absolutely hates the place, and is terrified every time someone comes near her.

Bronchiolitis is not a terribly uncommon ailment for wee kids, but once again, not many of them seem to get hit quite as hard as Katie does. Poor thing, she sounds like she's been smoking 20 a day for 40 years. Her sleep is awful, she feels dreadful, and the cough keeps waking her up even when she does get to sleep. Another thing you have to watch out for with bronchiolitis, is that they can become congested in the middle of the night, and stop breathing. We find that she actually sleeps a little better slightly elevated, almost sitting up. During the day that's fine, as we can sit on the couch with her slouching on us, watching some of her TV shows, Balamory, or the fucking Wiggles…. don't get me started on the fucking Wiggles.

Anyway, we try to get her to sleep with us at night but she is having none of it, so we put a mattress on the floor of her room, and 'sleep' there ourselves, checking on her every half hour, taking turns for about four nights. We buy a humidifier, which is supposed to help her breathe better, and we often go into the shower room and turn all the hot taps on until it steams up. If she is having a strong coughing fit, that works quite well.

At the end of four days, when we finally emerge from this particular hell I take some photos of the room we have been living in—and it looks like a crack den! It is actually quite funny, the state of the place, and the fact that we hadn't even noticed. But hey, we all make it through and I might be able to laugh about it, one day.

Another time at the hospital, a doctor tells us there are kids who get sick six times a year, and kids who get sick 26 times a year, and it looks like we're in category two. Then she proceeds to inform us that we have about a year of this shit ahead.

Not the words she uses but that's what I heard, and it's longer than a year actually, but by then, who the hell is counting the days anymore.

In and out of hospital as often as we are however, I always feel comfortable when we get there, and we always receive excellent treatment. You feel in safe hands, and you are also exposed to children who have real problems.

Kids on dialysis machines, kids with tubes sticking out all over the place, kids with cancer, paramedics rushing by with kids on trolleys, tiny kids with god knows what wrong with them. A hell of a place to gain perspective. We're not so bad off.

Nevertheless, it's pretty hard work overall, and, we begin to think about moving home…

Our anniversary arrives and I book tickets to the Opera House, to see the Sydney Symphony Orchestra perform Handel's 'The Planets', accompanied by HD images from NASA on a large screen. Should be a lovely evening, but we both almost fall asleep during the show, and afterwards discuss packing it all in and moving home. To Ireland probably, where Erin's expansive family can help us out.

If it continues to be this difficult why the hell *should* we stay on the other side of the world where there's nobody to help. It is the first time I think that, although I know Erin has been keen to move back for a while.

We decide to give it a year, and if we are still struggling, then that's it—we'll go back to Ireland. It's family you need. They're the only people you can count on when this kind of shit is going down– if you're lucky that is. Grannies to take the kid off your hands for two hours of a Sunday afternoon. Just enough to help you keep your sanity.

What we really need is for Erin's sister, Niamh, to mind Katie during the day now and again. Erin is reluctant to ask though, and I don't want to interfere. Niamh has her own life and we don't want to impose upon her too much. She's done the odd Friday night, allowing us out for a bite to eat, but we're so bloody knackered, all we really want to do is sleep in the evenings.

However, after our anniversary 'we need to think about heading home' discussion, I decide to have a word with Niamh. I'm not so subtle about these sorts of things, and when I tell her we are in trouble and need some help, she is only too happy to pitch in. She had actually been trying to help out as much as possible, but didn't know what to do. Didn't want to impose too much. Ha! Anyway, another lesson learned. Don't be afraid to ask for help.

It also begins to dawn on us, that while we think we have a good little baby, perhaps we don't. Sleep, reflux, crying when she eats, now all the illness. Fuck, just as well she's a bloody cutie!

Dealing with illness: My facts

Never easy, but gets easier with experience, and if you're armed with the facts it's less frightening. After a couple of times into hospital with Katie in the middle of the night I asked one of the nurses to give me all the 'Fact Sheets' they had. Everything that could go wrong with a kid. She was reluctant to hand them over to me and I had to reassure her I wasn't a nut case, or a transposing hypochondriac (I think I just made that expression up).

Here's a shortlist of the most common ailments. Bronchiolitis, Bacterial infection, Viral infection, Fever, Sore ears, Gooey eye, Conjunctivitis, Gastroenteritis, Foot and mouth disease, Urinary Tract Infection, Cold & Flu, Dehydration, Tummy bug, Teething.

Except for Foot and Mouth disease Katie got them all, numerous times. In general, this is how we dealt with an illness. Although I hasten to add that anything you read here is only what *we* did, with Katie. All children are different. Should you do what I mention here and something untoward happens to your child, it's all on you.

First sign of illness
Was generally a temperature. Remember a high temperature is the body's way of making the environment less appealing to any of the nasties that might have invaded.

So you need to let it stay a wee bit high, but not so much that your kid is completely buggered. You'll know yourself when your child has reached this stage. With Katie, she could carry a reasonably high temperature without too much of an issue, but when she became sluggish, and only wanted to lie down in your arms as opposed to shifting around all over the place, we knew it was time to do something.

There are three ways to lower a temperature. Taking off clothes and cooling the body, taking Paracetamol and taking Nurofen.

First of all we'd take her clothes off, see if that helped for a while, but inevitably we'd have to move on to Paracetamol.

At any point in time, if she went to sleep we'd just keep an eye on her, and try to keep the room cool. We would never wake her up just to give her more Paracetamol or Nurofen, but, if she was so hot she couldn't sleep properly, then we'd give her one or the other.

The temperature, of course, is only a symptom of something else going on. Either a virus of some sort, or a bacteria. With a virus there's nothing you can do about it, with a bacteria, antibiotics can generally help out. So, if the fever didn't clear in a couple of days, we'd go to the doctor. If they suspected it was bacterial they'd prescribe antibiotics, and we'd be off on a course of Amoxicillin probably. If it was a virus, you just have to keep them as comfortable as possible until the body fights it off.

That's pretty much it, for almost every illness. Keep an eye on them yourself to begin with, if it gets really bad go to hospital, if it's not too bad but seems to hang around for a long time, go to the doctors.

Despite all our unanswered questions about Katie's underlying issues, I must admit the medical fraternity were great in dealing with all of these little infections.

When she is well enough in amongst all this illness, she is off to childcare. The drop off in the morning is my job, and this is how it plays out.

I wake at 6:20am, shower, change and get ready for work, maybe have a sip of coffee before waking Katie up at 7am. Of course she never sleeps in like this at the weekends. It takes her 10 minutes or so to wake up properly, and although I should enjoy waking her up when she isn't ready (she's certainly done it to us enough) I don't really. I put on 'The Best of Al Green', and then we begin. It's nice, I like this part of the morning, it is only further on that the wheels fall off and I want to kill myself, but right now it's all good. As the man says 'I'm so in love with you, whatever you want to do, is alright with meeeeeeee.'

Task 1. Nappy change. This has become almost impossible — she just won't stay on her back, spins over as soon as you whip her nappy off—shite all over the place if you're not careful. I give her a pot of Vaseline to play with, and then off with the breeches—wipe, cream, nappy on—done. Nappy in the bag—in the bin—clean hands—ready for the next step.

Task 2. Clean gunk out of her eye—and brush our teeth. She's had a blocked tear duct since she was born which means there's a permanent build up of yellowy pus in the corner of her eye. When she wakes up sometimes, it is so hard packed that she can't even open it. We're seeing a series of specialists about that too, and for now the plan is to keep cleaning it and hope it unblocks itself, before having to resort to surgery. So, I clean her eye, then we both brush our teeth and we're back into the living room. I drop her down on the big rug and hop into the kitchen.

Task 3. Breakfast. So far so good. Breakfast is either porridge or baby rice, and as an accredited master of organisation Erin has blended loads of fruit and frozen them into ice cube trays, then deposited them into labeled bags in the freezer. I stick a fruity ice cube into the porridge and stir it through to cool it down, give it a bit of flavour, and hey presto—porridge that she might even eat.

This is when the morning takes a turn for the worse. I pick her up and sit her in the baby chair, which is stuffed full of cushions because she's still so small, then I try and feed the little bugger. I pile up some books for her to play with, a spoon for her to wave around (not actually eat with of course) and nearby I have a little pot of breakfast cereal.

So the scene is set—bring on the kid. She takes the first mouthful of food from me, then virtually every single mouthful after that, is a freakin' fight to the death. A fight that she wins almost every morning.

At some point the books are swept off the table, could be either one of us by this stage, and I take the opportunity to replace them with some breakfast cereal, which she strikes at like a Praying Mantis. She is pretty good at this bit, they're maneuvered into the mouth quick style, and while she is at it I can usually jam another mouthful of porridge into her. Ha ha!

Unimpressed with my sneaky move, she now wriggles down in the chair, so that her arms stick up beside her ears, and she's about to fall through the bottom of the feckin' thing. This is accompanied by groans of frustration, not mine I hasten to add, I've moved on to more advanced emotions by now. Anyway this is her way of letting me know she's had enough of this charade, and it is time to get the hell out of the chair.

I know how she feels. I want to get the fuck out of here too—in fact that's the bloody problem. Having moved on emotionally from frustration. I have graduated into anger and disbelief. "Aaaagh eat the freakin' food—aaaagh look how late I'm going to be for work—aaaagh how on earth did I let this happen again—aaagh." You get the picture.

So anyway, out the chair and she's all smiles again. My anger, frustration and all the rest of it fades, not completely, but almost. Now is probably the time that I'd like to be walking out of the door, except we've got tasks four, five, six, and if I'm unlucky, number seven too.

Task 4. Wash her hands and face cause the little tike's a mess.

Task 5. Get her dressed. I pick her up to sit on my knee, facing away in case she throws up what little food she's eaten. Grab a good value toy to amuse her, keep her hands busy—keys, some type of lotion or socks are usually winners here. Then it's time to take off her pajamas. Off with the, now covered-in-food, onesie and on with a new one. On with the trousers, on with a top, socks, a jumper, and last of all a big puffy jacket. Estimated time for of all of that—anywhere from 4-7 minutes.

Task 6. The bag. We're almost out the door—just make

sure everything required is in her 'day care' bag. Again Erin is very organised with this, god love her, and the bag is already packed with a little note sitting on top detailing any last minute items I might need to add.

A yoghurt—in case she doesn't eat anything at childcare (cause she'll almost always eat yoghurt), her sleeping bag, and the most important item in her life, and hence ours too—Zulu, her security blanket Giraffe. It's actually so important to calming her down that we've purchased five identical Zulus. Task six complete, we head off down to the car, unless of course…

Task 7. This often happens just I am finished getting her dressed—fuck—another nappy change required. Fuck sake.

Finally we're out the front door and she's smiling at me again. I push aside the fact that I'm late for work, and comfort myself with the knowledge that there's no more important job in the world, than the one I'm doing right now. I get her in the baby seat, close the door and wave through the window—another smile. This is why the human race is still around. These smiles.

Off to childcare and I expect her to start kicking up a fuss, but she doesn't. She saves that for the very moment that one of the ladies takes her from me. There's a little panic, we struggle off with her jacket—and I go through the list of instructions for the day. I'm never entirely sure these are followed. I can't remember all the instructions myself—they're always scribbled down or on my phone.

Anyway, that's it, job done. They wander over to some toys, I say good-bye and then put her bag in the locker.

I try and catch a glimpse of her without any tears, and once I get it I'm off to work holding that memory in my mind. Sometimes however, she sees me at the window and then I'm off to work with an entirely different picture. One

I'd rather not have—her face full of panic, or even worse the accusatory look—the 'how can you leave me here' look. By the time I get back down the elevator, it's actually time to start work, except I've still got to drive half way across the city. Text to my boss, on my way, sorry I'm late—and off I go.

So that's it. Three days a week. Tuesday, Thursday and Friday.

Now that reminds me, talking of frustration—not sure if I've mentioned as yet but if you've ever found yourself sitting around, waiting to get out the door because your good lady is taking her time getting ready—wait until you have a fucking kid. It is absolutely unbe-fucking-lievable, how long it takes to get out the house when you have a little one. It gets better later on, but at this stage—Oh My God. Anyway, enough said. Just wait and see.

iPhone Notes—From Erin for Childcare
—No safety sleep
—StN up routine
—1:15-1:30 in morning
—1 hr in afternoon
—Try and resettle
—2.5 hours awake
—Toy and book before sweets at meal—unless very upset
—Water before sleep & with meal
—Letter for eye
—Pick up at?
—Teething a bit

iPhone Notes—My translation

—No safety sleep - *I can't remember what this means.*
—StN up routine - *Nor this.*
—1:15-1:30 in morning - *Nope.*
—1 hr in afternoon - *Tell them we're aiming for Katie to sleep about an hour in the afternoon.*
—Try and resettle - *If she doesn't sleep for an hour, try and re-settle her.*
—2.5 hours awake - *She was awake for 2.5 hours in the middle of the night, so she should be tired and she'll really need her sleep—so please take heed of what I've just said.*
—Toy and book before sweets at meal—unless very upset - *During lunch time, she generally eats better if you put some toys, and a book or two on her table. Best to do this before any pudding or sweet treats arrive. If she's very upset however, don't bother with this, as it will have no effect at all.*
—Water before sleep & with meal - *She likes a bit of water before she goes to sleep, this can often help her get her head down, and she likes a bit of water with lunch too.*
—Letter for eye - *As per your request, we've asked the doctor for a letter saying that her 'gooey eye' isn't conjunctivitis, hence not infectious and putting other kids at risk. It hasn't arrived yet, but I'll get it to you as soon as it does.*
—Pick up at? - *When shall we pick her up today?*
—Teething a bit - *She's teething a bit (so eating and sleeping is going to be even more difficult than usual!) ... Good luck!*

Given the fact that they have about 50 different kids in there, I'd say they have virtually zero chance of remembering any of this.

Unsurprisingly, during this time of constantly being at work or at home, looking after the wee one who is invariably ill, I begin to feel as if it is all getting on top of me again.

Thanks to a dream run at the traffic lights I get to work

a wee bit early one day, and I find myself with 10 minutes of free time. 10 delightful minutes where I put the car seat back, find some music on the stereo and briefly close my system down. It's a beautiful stolen moment, and in reality I feel as if I need about a week of this—happy to take the 10 minutes though.

Despite the fact that I'm losing my enthusiasm and drive a little, I find I'm actually becoming incredibly efficient. What I have on my plate, combined with the fact that I never have a moment to myself, has turned me into a freakin' machine. I'm unbelievably intolerant of anyone who is, in my mind, wasting my time. Time thieves I call them. For example, when a project manager producing a website for me calls and rambles on about how she doesn't think they can do what I've asked, she's not sure yet, but blah de blah de blah… I just cut her off there and then. Quite uncharacteristically so. I'm normally quite sociable at work, happy to have a bit of conversation around a business matter, but not this time.

"Let me just stop you right there. Is this a problem yet? Do you know for sure that you can't do it yet? No? Well go and find out, work through it all, and only come back to me if there's a problem, OK?"

My colleague comments "Iain, that was brilliant!". "I just don't have any time for pussy footing around Linda." She's got two kids, she understands.

Erin is feeling the strain too, so we decide to have a go at getting our lives back. A morning off every other weekend is the plan. Do with it what you wish, but the most important part, is that it has to be a guilt free pass.

We seem to have ended up in a strange situation, where we are scared of leaving each other to face the music alone for too long. So neither of us ever gets the break we need. I'm in an office five days a week, and at the weekends I want to try and give Erin a rest, so I can hardly bugger off for a surf, a hike, or, you know, have a life. Erin is the same. Although I'll take Katie out at the weekends and let her catch up on some sleep, she doesn't want to take too much time to herself. She doesn't want me to have to deal with Katie on my own for my only two days off.

Anyway, the 'one morning to yourself, every other weekend' policy begins to pay dividends. And slowly, for a while at least we start to feel a bit more human.

Lots of people I know have run into this kind of problem, where they don't want to leave their partners to 'deal with it all' so in the end, nobody ever gets a break. I think if you're living near family or a great support network you'd probably never encounter this kind of nonsense. But there you go, we're the ones who wanted to come and live in Australia, so we just have to suck it up.

Despite the story I'm telling here of illness, exhaustion and lack of mojo, there are lots of great times in amongst all this too. Like when Erin and Katie meet me off the train from work one day and we head down to a little Dumpling House in Chinatown. Before too long Katie has charmed the ladies into a wee dance with her in the middle, all hands waving and clapping—loving it so she is.

In the park one beautiful sunny day, she is swamped by a flurry of Scotty dogs, and down at the Fish Markets one afternoon with her Aunty Niamh when she gets up close and personal with some seagulls. She does seem to have a way with animals this little lady. Dancing in the living room and trying to play the ukulele, even though it's about the same size as her. All great stuff. Lovely moments.

On the health front, we've now been advised that it might be her ears that are causing the problems. She frequently has earache, and with all the swimming in my past I know exactly what that's like—it's bloody agony. The doctor has started talking about grommets, which I've never heard of before, but don't like the sound of in the least.

The theory is, because Katie has been ill for about four months now—with a constantly running nose—the 'goo' has backed up her nasal passages and spilled over into her inner ear. Once there it will drain out, eventually, but not if it's being topped up all the time, as it is in this case. Gunk in your inner ear for months at a time quickly becomes a breeding ground for bacteria, and hence, Katie's constant earache.

So, to the grommets—this is where they pierce a hole in the eardrum to drain out the gunk, then put a little 'grommet' in there to keep the eardrum open, draining it on a continuous basis.

They leave it in there for six months or so, then you go back to the doctors to see if the infection has gone, pull the grommets out and the eardrum seals over. Apart from the obvious fact that putting a hole in your eardrum sounds like a fucking awful thing to do (it's surgery to get them in there) there are a number of other factors that make it something to avoid if possible.

You can't let any water get in their ears for six months, so there's no swimming, no beach, and you have to be careful in the bath. Later on in life they might have trouble equalizing, which means that flying and scuba diving could be a major problem.

Needless to say, we do not want to go down the grommet route until we have absolutely no choice in the matter. We decide to park it for a while, see if we can get rid of her permanent cold first.

And thank god we did. Her ears were bad sure enough, but eventually they cleared without us having to hammer a spike through her eardrum.

The ongoing costs of parenthood: My facts

Now's as good a time as any to address the cost of all of this. Another quip I remember throwing to people about to have a baby, was not to forget the opportunity cost, of what you 'thought' you were going to do with the rest of your life. I really was an asshole back then, probably still the case sometimes. Anyway, childcare for example, even when they don't go (because they're ill) costs about $100 a day. And a medical specialist and doctors? They can write their own ticket. With a sick kid at home, you'll pay any amount to fix 'em.

Not including set-up costs, this is what it cost us, up until Katie's first birthday. I didn't keep account of it at the time so the accuracy might be a little sketchy, but it's a guide at least. I've tried to recall, or estimate every single expense apart from food. Costs are obviously going to vary widely depending on your baby's needs. I think our medical expenses were probably more than most for example, but you never know what's going to happen, and I'm sure they were also a hell of a lot less than they could have been.

Nappies:
- On average for the first year, probably looking at about four nappies a day, which is 1,460 nappies. 90 in a box of Huggies that costs $33.

—Total cost: $561

Nappy bags:
- Scented little plastic bags that you stick a dirty nappy in, then tie up and pop in the bin. You *never* want to run out of these. 1,460 required. 50 in a box that costs $2

—Total cost: $60

Wipes:
- You *never* want to run out of these either. Estimate about one pack (80 wipes) a week. Plus a few little packs that go in the car, and in bags etc…

—Total cost: $300

Formula:
- We didn't start Katie on Formula until she was about six months old. Regular Formula is $23, and it would last a week.

—Total cost: $598

Medical Expenses:
- Because we weren't too sure what was wrong with Katie, we were constantly visiting different types of practitioners to see who could help us out. This is what I remember from that first year, although I'm sure it's not all covered here, and realistically a lot more costs piled up in year two.
- Naturopath: $90 x 5 —$450
- Naturopathic medicine: $300
- Homeopath: $90 x 5 —$450
- Homeopathic medicine: $200
- Acupuncturist: $90 x 5 —$450
- Prescribed medicine: $300
- Other 'medical' expenses:
- Humidifier-to help with Katie's breathing and cough—$43
- Eucalyptus oil for humidifier—$7, x 2 = $14
- Heater—storage heater for Katie's room—$50
- Bonjela—$8
- Teething powder—$11
- Teething chews—3 x $7 = $21

- Super nanny—$900
- Baby Books—$100
- Door closing hooks—$30
- Rounded table corner protectors—$6
- Nose clearing solution—$8
- Bepampethan—$9
- Curash Powder—$6
- Baby Panadol—$4
- Baby Nurofen—$7
- Paracetamol suppositories—$10
- Thermometer—Braun ear thermometer—$97
- Underarm thermometer—$7
- Mouth thermometer—$7
- Replacement covers for ear thermometer—$14

Childcare:
- The first place we managed to get Katie into charged $100 a day, and the Government paid half. Erin had a year off work so we had only *just* started putting her in there for three days a week towards the end of the year. Three days, at $50 a day, for two months.

—Total cost: $1,200

Clothes:
- As they grow so quickly they're constantly outgrowing things. On the other hand, most of their clothes don't cost a fortune—but watch out for the shoes!
- This is a considered guess, but roughly you're looking at three different 'sizes' in the first year, and you'll need a whole new wardrobe for each size:
- Shoes, socks, leggings, jeans, tracksuit pants, vests, long sleeve tops, jumpers, jackets, hats, sleeping suit, onesies.

- 0-3 months (already paid for in set up costs)
- 3-6 months—$300
- 6-9 months—$400
- 9-12 months—$500

—Total cost: $1,200

Toys:
- You can't put a price on this. I found it difficult to go anywhere without buying a little something. We steered away from bombarding Katie with a lot of 'big ticket' items, but probably went overboard with the small bits and pieces and books, which I never mind buying though.

—Total cost: $800 (total guess)

Shit you don't need:
- $50-$5,000+… up to you and your missus

Travel cot:
- Very useful, but unbelievably complicated to put up and down. Good luck.

—Total cost: $70

Travel expenses:
- We took Katie back to Ireland and Scotland, but kids are free until they turn two. Just so you know, you have to complete the return journey before their second birthday, or you'll get hit with an *almost* full fare.
- Wraps for swaddling And blankets. Probably bought another seven or eight of these.

—Total cost: $150

Other stuff:
- External hard drive, to handle the thousands of photographs we were generating with our iPhones on a daily basis—$170
- Ikea mat and hanging things, for Katie to lie on and play with swinging toys—we've still got this mat, and use it every day—$25
- Two tyre repairs on the pram—$30 each!
- A hand pump for the pram—$7
- Car seat mirror, so she could see herself—$25
- Sippy cups—$6 x 3 = $18
- Bowls—$30
- Plates—$20
- Cutlery—$12
- Dummy—$9

Stuff that goes in the bathroom:
- Shampoo—Aveeno baby shampoo—3 x $10 = $30
- Vaseline—2 x $15 = $30
- Sudocrem—2 x $22 = $44
- Paw paw ointment—2 x $20 = $40
- Pocket hankies—20 packets—$2 each = $40
- Box hankies—20 packets—$2 each = $40
- Sun Cream—2 x $8 = $16
- Ear cleaning things—$4
- Eye pads—$12
- Antibacterial gel—$7

So, total set-up costs were $3,291, plus ongoing costs of $9,280 up to the first birthday party = $12,571. Kids. Not cheap, but then again *supposed* to be so worth it. You certainly don't hear of people on their deathbed wishing they had spent more time with their money.

28

Eleven Months: Back To Reality

"Before I got married I had six theories about bringing up children, now I have six children, and no theories."
— Jon Wilmot. **Six children!**

It's the wettest July in 23 years apparently. Took me over an hour to drive home last night, even with a few illegal moves thrown in.

So the bus today and the train, then I'll run home from Central Station. Don't care if it's raining. I didn't see Katie last night because of the weather, or the night before because of another idiot who couldn't drive and held me up.

I'd rather run, get wet, and see Katie. Plus I'll probably get some strange kind of joy running around in the pouring rain. Especially when everyone else is trapped in their little tin cans, stuck in traffic going nowhere, stuck in their little lives. Stuck. Fuck. "Aaaaaarrrgggghh… I'm freeeee! Fuuuuck. Fuck you aaaaaall." Ahem. Excuse me.

So, Erin and I were up for about an hour last night, around 3am to 4am. Little lady is still having problems settling because of her cough, her cold, and whatever the fuck else she has. Pretty knackered when I woke up this morning.

She had another week off childcare too, and now the deadline for Erin going back to work is hurtling towards us at a frightening pace. She's only done one full week so far, so we're a bit nervous about what happens when they keep sending her home and we're at work. Only so many days you can take off, so I've signed up for a baby sitting service - people who can pick her up if we're strapped.

$30 an hour... not shockingly bad, although if it turns out we need a full time nanny that means around $240 a day. Let's hope we don't have to go down that route... if we do, it's not really worth Erin going back to work at all.

I get the train back to Central and run home as planned, but it isn't raining. I'm actually a bit disappointed. "Aaaaaagh Fuuuuuuucck"—I would have enjoyed that. Ah well, best laid plans gang aft astray.

In fact, all plans have been going astray since Katie joined us. From the moment she arrived in this world she's set her own agenda, and we've all been following along. Even the timing of her arrival—three weeks early, and then 40 hours to come out.

She certainly likes to keep you on your toes. Never too predictable. One morning I find myself an unexpected recipient of a little bit of 'me' time. I'm up and ready before Katie is, and she sleeps in a bit, so I put some nice music on and sit there quietly looking at the city—steam drifting up over the skyline as the sun begins to take the chill out of the air.

I have a coffee sitting beside me, and I manage to drink most of it for a change. A clear crisp day. 7:11am. Wait 'till we see if she puts a spanner in the works. She's been in particularly good form lately, great fun, and although her nose is still running (that's about four months now) and she's still got a horrible cough, she's in good health. 7:14am. Ahhh. Peace... Oh, there she is.

It's Erin's last week before she starts work. I hope she manages to enjoy a few days of free time before she's back into it all again. And talk about timing, at this last minute before she does return to the workplace, Katie finally manages to string a few good days together at childcare.

She sleeps well, eats and plays well—at last. Then she takes her first proper steps there too. What a shame neither of us are around to see it, but there are more steps later on that evening at home. We had already reorganised the house when she started to pull herself up on things. Ornaments, picture frames, lamps—all of them had to go before she pulled them down on top of herself. It does help being organised. You can make your life a hell of a lot easier with a wee one if you have a plan. My childcare run in the morning for example—I don't have it down pat just yet, but I'm getting there, refining the process every day and it *is* becoming easier.

Back to work, back to life

Erin finally returns to work in early August, having been off for a year although only nine months had been planned for. That same day, I take Katie to childcare and make it into work on time, for the first time ever. Later on, Erin picks Katie up on her way home and as simple as that, we transform into a working family.

Erin describes going back to work as horrific. Awful. Katie has a serious case of separation anxiety and although it is me who drops her off, Erin feels it. She is also getting very little sleep, then has to go into work and 'prove' that she can still do the job despite the fact she is now a mother. Katie's constant illnesses add to the difficulty and there's the additional stress involved when we both have to take time off work to look after her.

Now we've joined the human race for sure. And I guess the hope is, that we haven't just joined the rat race. It's funny though. I used to think that I never wanted to do the usual thing, bring up kids, get a mortgage, work a 9-5 Monday to Friday job. And I still don't think that's me, but, I'm also very aware now, that it's hardly anyone. People just do what they have to do, to get by, because they love their children and want the best for them. And also you know what? It 'aint so bad for a wee while.

Oh yeah sometimes I want to kill people. There's ups and downs in every workplace, and bullshit that nobody should have to put up with but hey, that's life. Deal with it or get a job where nobody gives a fuck. Unfortunately those jobs tend to pay fuck all too.

I manage to enjoy what I do most of the time. Even if it's not exactly what I think I 'should' be doing. And I think one of the keys to happiness, is acceptance. Learning to be happy with what you've got, not constantly pining for something new. I say this now, calmly sitting here at peace. I don't always think this way, but at least I know I should try.

Unless you're one of the lucky people who get to do what you love for a living, and it happens to pay rather well too, you're probably in the same boat as me. Doing the best you can, having good days and bad, trying to put some money aside for your future, or your kids. Here's an irony I suspect is ahead. I haven't reached it yet but I think it's a distinct possibility.

In order to reach that point in your life, where you're successful enough to be able to do whatever you want, you've no doubt had to get used to doing a whole load of shit you don't like. In fact you've had to do so much of it, that your brain has developed a coping mechanism to deal with it. The mechanism that tells you to shut the fuck up—either change your situation, or find the pleasure in what you're doing, and quit your bloody whingeing. And you know that voice is right, because otherwise you're going to be depressed on a permanent basis, and who wants to live like that?!

And so, when you finally get to the stage where you're free to do anything, you're actually not that bothered about what you're doing at that point in time anyway—because you've taught yourself to suck it up, get on with it—and find the joy. I don't know for sure, but it wouldn't surprise me if this little nugget of truth is just sitting there, waiting for me to trip over it in about 20 years or so.

We make a list for Katie's first birthday party; 25 adults, 6 kids, 12 noon on a Sunday, champagne and cake. Rock 'n roll. All paper and plastic cups in the park so we can bin everything afterwards and nothing gets broken—how disgustingly mature and fucking sensible.

29

Twelve Months: Down And Almost Out

"You can learn many things from children. How much patience you have, for instance."
—Franklin P. Adams. **True, but there is more.**

The twelfth month for Katie is all about walking. Now I know why they're called toddlers. She swaggers around the house like a drunken little John Wayne. It's hilarious—and she is so happy as she pieces together longer and longer trips before falling on her bum. Her first couple of steps quickly develop into four, then five, and eventually there is no stopping her.

She is walking when we go to our first, 1st birthday party—a little fella she met through Erin's mothers group.

I am so proud of her. She is so content, just doddling around on her own, going up to people and saying hello. I wander around myself, keeping my distance but keeping an eye on her. Enjoying her curious nature in these overcrowded and foreign surroundings. She toddles into the bathroom and says hello to a 'not-so-little' little girl. Then the little girl pulls her hair, and I could slap the bugger.

I hold back, of course, summoning the energy to subdue my fatherly instincts, and watch with interest to see how Katie deals with it. So I watch, and as I wait for her to get upset or respond in kind (like I would have done), nothing happens. She just looks at this little kid for a moment, looks at something else that catches her attention, and then wanders off. Again I'm incredibly proud. She just wasn't bothered, couldn't give a shit. 'Ah well you do what you like. I'm off to check out this shiny ornament over here—cheerio.' Of course this is nonsense. However I can't help projecting my own emotions, my own (wishful) thoughts on to her, guessing at what she might be thinking. Probably says more about me than her. I thought I knew a thing or two? Here I am learning tolerance from my 11-month-old daughter. I could do with taking it easy a little bit more often.

We've also been told that the odd word won't be far away now either, so we try to stop swearing, and as Irish and Scottish people, we find it rather difficult. More so myself, truth be told, although I was pleased to overhear a comment from Erin the other day "Come on little lady, we'll set your high-chair up on the balcony—that might prevent the shit-fight for today..."

I learned to swear when I was three. My mum and dad went on holiday (to get a couple of night's sleep) and left me with my Aunty May, Uncle Andy, and my cousins Mark and Kim who were a wee bit older. Anyway, when they came back from the holiday their bags were all piled up in the hallway. I came out to say hello, tripped up over a bag and muttered "Oh, for fuck's sake". Shock, then hilarity ensued.

My Uncle Andy, and my dad, both swear like troopers. So I was fucked from the start as I suspect my daughter might be, but we do try to keep a lid on it. We're not in Glasgow anymore, and people in the rest of the world just don't swear quite as much as we do. I don't think a two year old wandering around telling people to go fuck themselves would go down very well in a Sydney childcare centre. Although deep down, I think I would find it hilarious.

Anyway, it seems like our little lady might be quite a sensitive soul. The three of us are sitting on the rug in the living room one morning, Katie has a leg hanging out of her PJs and she looks like 'Jake the Peg', so I sing the song and it turns out Erin has never heard it before. I go straight on to YouTube, and all three of us sit there watching Rolf Harris sing at one of the Royal Variety Shows. At the end of the song, one of the options that appears is another Rolf Harris number 'Two Little Boys'. Click. It's been ages since I've heard that song, and I remember it being a touching little number. In my state of exhaustion it just gets to me, and I shed a tear or two. What is even more touching than Rolf's story of war, brotherhood, loyalty and death however, is the fact that Katie reaches out for me. I'm convinced she knows that something is wrong with her daddy and wants to give me a cuddle. Well, for me to give her a cuddle really—but hey, let's not split hairs. It is a nice wee moment.

Health and hard times

Katie's health however, is not coming on as well as her sensitive side or the length of her stride. She continues to be ill most of the time, nothing dreadful, just colds, flu and viruses, but because of her spiking temperatures we often end up in hospital, and sleep is at an all time low.

We also have another 'change of opinion' on what her eating issues might be. We decide that it might actually be *our* problem, not Katie's. In other words it is basically down to our expectations. Expecting her to eat too much, and then getting upset because she doesn't. She is still tiny you see, so we want her to eat so she doesn't fall further below the 'percentile' curve. But now we are beginning to think that, hey, maybe she's just bloody small—and that's that.

We were right on that front actually. She was, and still is small. But this latest idea, that all we had to do was lower our expectations and all would be fine, couldn't have been further from the truth. I can't remember how many more opinions we had, or had to listen to, before we finally got to the bottom of it all. It took us another six months or so, but eventually, we discovered that the underlying cause of absolutely everything— the crying, the eating, the lack of sleep, the slow rate of growth and the permanent illnesses—all of it was due to food intolerances.

Something I'd never even heard of before, and I wish that was still the case. A food intolerance is kind of like a milder form of an allergy. There's a whole world of it out there, and it's terrifying. You have no idea how much crap goes into the food we eat, and the reactions we're having to it.

I'm not going to get into all the details here, but basically, people react in different ways to the various chemicals in food. I'm not even talking processed foods here, I'm talking about naturally occurring chemicals, called salicylates and amines for example, that are in just about everything.

The reactions can be anything as simple as rashes and itchiness, through stomach pains, fatigue and sleeplessness, all the way through to mood swings and learning difficulties. The onset of the symptom depends on how much an individual can tolerate, before the reaction is tipped.

Katie had issues with dairy, salicylates, and amines, and she had very low tolerance levels. When she was only a couple of months old, and would cry for ages after a feed for example, she was reacting to the food in her mother's milk. We had actually noticed that when Erin ate garlic, the crying was worse, so we'd taken it out of her diet but had failed to make the connection between this and everything else.

The constant illnesses were a result of this too. As Katie ingested anything that her body couldn't tolerate, it was like a poison, so her immune system had to go to work fighting off the toxins. This meant that she had very few defences left to deal with other intruders, such as bacteria and viruses, which is why she caught every single bug that was going, and caught it hard.

As for the sleeping, well, considering we were literally poisoning her about five times a day, I'm not surprised she was a little distressed and couldn't put her head down for too long. Food intolerances were buggering it all up, and for the first year and a half of her life, nobody had a bloody clue.

Dealing with a kid who has intolerances is a subject in its own right, so I won't go into it any more right now, but if you think you're up against something that sounds like this, there's a whole load of websites out there full of people all going through the same shit. Low salicylate recipes and all sorts of stuff, Erin became addicted to these for a while. A good book to read is Fed Up *by Sue Dengate, and if you really want, drop me a line. I'd be happy to help out if I can.*

Anyway, we were still months away from figuring all of this out, and approaching her 1st birthday party we were really just stumbling around in the dark. Quite literally. We were up 10 times in one evening I remember, and sleep was once again a rare commodity. Now and again you'd almost get out of the fugue of tiredness, then she'd have another bad night.

Perspective ...

And just when you think everything sucks, and how could it get any worse, life has a tendency of showing you why you need to shut the fuck up, and enjoy what you've got. There is a lot going on outside of our little family that helps put things in perspective yet again—serious illness, of the life threatening variety in people far too young to be facing such things. A great friend of Erin's has just had a pretty awful cancer scare. She is only 37, and when you think about things like that, well, you've just got to enjoy every day, and appreciate what's in front of you.

And so, eventually, we make it to Katie's first birthday party. A day that it seemed would never come. Breathe in…. fwhooo…. breathe out…. phhhooooo. I really do see it as a 'crossing the finish line' moment. What we've been through to get to this stage, I can hardly believe.

A 40-hour marathon birth that still traumatises me when I think about it. An amazing child with the most powerful lungs you could possibly imagine. Skin tags, grommets, Benjamin Bratt, dream feeds, Nanny McPhee, finance wankers, mudskipping, a frightening insight into the torture industry and an unbelievable, visceral launch into the real world. Brain aneurisms, cancer, love, life, Valentine's day, New Idea magazines, 60,000 fucking baby names, growth, pain, tolerance, worry, round the world and back again and a learning curve you wouldn't believe.

But we made it, all three of us, as a family. Thank goodness. We still don't understand all of Katie's issues, but we are getting there. Erin and I have had our differences, but we've managed through. And here we are—our little girl is one.

The weather is touch and go, so we have the party in our apartment instead of the park out front. There are around 20 people, half a dozen kids and Katie in a purple party dress her granny sent from Scotland. Katie gorges herself on chocolate cake (which she would never have eaten normally) and runs about the place totally high on sugar, and totally high on the attention. A superstar. A proud and exhausted mum and dad.

A year down, with lots more to go, and looking forward to every sleepless moment of it.

30

And We're Only Getting Started …

> *"Embrace your beautiful mess of a life with your child. No matter how hard it gets, do not disengage. Do something—anything—to connect with and guide your child today. Parenting is an adventure of the greatest significance. It is your legacy."*
> —Andy Kerckhoff. **Aye, and it's exhausting too.**

So there you go, that's my story. That was two, maybe three years of my life. The most exhilarating and exhausting adventure I've ever had.

This is how it all started falling into place.

1. Illness   Katie's permanent illnesses; colds, flus, lung infections, croup, you name it, all began to recede a little bit as she was approaching two. She'd been out of day care for quite a long time, hadn't been mixing with other kids and their germs, and her defences had finally had time to build themselves up. We were also getting on top of the food intolerances, so we weren't poisoning our little lady quite so much anymore.

2. Sleep   At the age of about two and a half, Katie slept through the night, and began to make a habit of it. As you can imagine this was a life-changing event, probably more so for Erin and I, than for Katie.

3. Food   About the same time her food tolerance issues seemed to ease too. She started eating all sort of things she never would have touched before, and stopped reacting to things that would have previously tipped her over the edge. Not only could we relax about what Katie ate right now, but our fears of her entire life being dominated by these restrictive dietary conditions, began to recede too.

4. Daycare   The final piece of the puzzle was daycare. We had a few false starts on this front. In and out of the first centre because of illness and food. Then we had a full time nanny for a while, but that was unsustainable financially. Next, Katie was accepted into the Family Day Care scheme (where someone looks after a few kids in their home) but it just didn't work out. And then, finally, Katie got a spot in a little day care centre round the corner from where we live. They catered to her dietary needs and they had a small number of kids, so could keep an eye on her properly. Within weeks she was used to the place, and within months she was totally at ease.

The difference this alone made in all of our lives was unbelievable. I don't think Erin and I actually realised quite how much pressure we were feeling, and how unhappy we were while Katie's day care situation was unresolved.

After daycare started working, everything in life became easier. We finally started living the 'family life' we wanted, and hoped, was waiting for us.

She adores going there now, she's got lots of wee pals who all live locally, and we've started getting to know all the parents too. All young families living nearby, and we feel much more at home in the community now too. They say it takes a village to bring up a child, we finally seem to be finding ours.

What I had been afraid of, really, was change. Yet change is inevitable, and best embraced I think. And adventure, well, I reckon it's all a matter of attitude, and timing. The great pioneers of the world, the people who went further, higher, deeper than anyone else, who broke down barriers of knowledge and convention—not that I compare myself to these folks by any stretch of the imagination—but most of them had kids too. And for a while I'm sure they were quite happy going no further than the local café for a piece of cake and a cup of tea, before heading home to look after their little one. It's just timing.

And realistically, there's no greater adventure than this. If you enjoy the random nature of life, blowing in the wind and going where the world takes you, well, this trip will take you places you never thought you would go. With the right attitude, you'll find things out about yourself you never would have guessed at, and believe me, it's the most unexpected random fucking thing there is.

My advice if you've read this far, would be to do whatever you've been 'thinking about' doing for a while now—learn the guitar, go climbing in the Himalayas or diving in Palau—then man up, and go have a baby.

Chances are your experience will be a lot easier than ours. Most kids eat and sleep without a fight, and most of them don't cry seemingly non-stop. But even if you do have some issues, overall it's just bumps in the road. Throughout all the exhaustion, the worry, the discontent and sometimes disbelief at what was happening in that first, and second year—all I had to do to make it better was to stop. Breathe. Take a break, and when everyone had calmed down—take a look at my daughter's face. That's what makes it all worthwhile. That's what keeps us all going.

And unfortunately, that's the most difficult part to put into words. I've tried my best, but at the end of the day you just have to take a leap of faith, get up on that feckin' bridge, and jump.

And trust me, it's amazing.

31

Epilogue: 40 Years Down

"Oh man! Look at those cavemen go. It's the freakiest show."
—David Bowie. **Sure feels like that sometimes.**

Ten years ago I had a fancy dress party for my 30th birthday. You had to come as someone famous, and everybody went to town with their costumes. I was Ziggy Stardust—sparkly make up and a leotard. Ha! What a sight. Afterwards about sixty or so of my 'closest friends' came back to my flat in Glasgow, where we carried on until about six the following morning. The police may have knocked on the door at some point. I can't remember, it was a fairly regular occurrence at that time in my life.

That was just before I moved to Sydney, and my recent 40th was a distinctly different affair. Instead of a night out, a party or a dinner, I wanted to spend a weekend away from the city, and I invited a slightly tighter group this time. 17 adults and six kids. I wanted to relax, spend some time with friends and avoid any fuss. Not really something that happens very much anymore.

We rented five cottages in a little holiday park north of the city. There was a pool, the beach nearby and outside in the middle of all the cottages, we set up a row of white plastic tables and chairs. Sitting there under the gum trees, sucking on a beer and surrounded by the smell of Aerogard, I couldn't imagine anything more Australian.

We had fish and chips out there one night, then Haggis Neeps and Tatties the next. Maybe a wee bit of a fuss *that* night, but hey. And some of us were still up at six in the morning, but that was because of the kids this time. Although I enjoyed catching up with friends I don't get to see very often, the best part was mucking around at the beach with the kids.

It was a great weekend. Erin was amazing, and did so much to make it all go smoothly, as did her sister Niamh. Katie meanwhile had an absolute ball, running around with all her little pals causing trouble, squeezing tomato ketchup all over the place, and generally having a fantastic time. In fact I heard her using that exact word, when she guided all the other kids toward the games room "Come on over here everybody, wait till you see in here… it's… it's…it's… FANTASTIC!"

Last weekend we took Katie to her first ballet class. As a bloke, it's not as if this was an event I'd been dreaming about, that I'd pictured in my mind and here it was finally happening. But I tell you what, it was fucking great. Katie was so pleased, and looked so cute in her little ballet outfit my heart could have burst.

I'm taking her swimming more often now. She's really getting into it—and we're just back from our first family holiday. This was the first time it's been just the three of us. We went to the Gold Coast. Spent countless hours in the swimming pool. Played mini-golf and even went to Sea World where we met Sponge Bob Square Pants and Dora the Explorer. She loved it almost as much as I did.

Katie is an absolute delight right now. She's such a funny, friendly, sensitive, outgoing, vibrant little girl you could hardly imagine all the heartache she's put us through. Not intentionally of course, but just all the difficulties we'd had with sleep, food and the rest of it. I keep reminding myself that the troubles we had are nothing compared to what lots of people have to face with their kids. But when you're in the middle of it, that's all there is. Nothing else counts, nothing else matters.

When I came home from work the other day Katie announced that she wanted the two of us to make a helicopter. "Oh… ah, OK" I said. We got the arts and crafts box out, Erin threw in an empty milk bottle and a cardboard box from the kitchen, and within 20 minutes we turned out a pretty cool helicopter. I must admit I was impressed myself. Katie must have been too, as I got a phone call from Erin the next morning telling me it had been carted off to daycare for 'show and tell'.

As they arrived, everyone began commenting on how amazing the helicopter was, and with each comment Katie's smile, and confidence grew just that little bit more as she basked in the glory of her achievements.

I was at work when I got the call from Erin, and much like Katie, it made my entire day. Nothing could touch me. I felt like the best dad in the world, and in the end, what's more important than that?

Ten weeks. Ten weeks!

PS. As I write there are only 10 weeks left until number two arrives. And although I'm not looking forward to the lack of sleep, and I know there will be tough times ahead, the thought of another wee person joining our family only brings a smile to my face.

Kind of like staring down the barrel of gun. Except you've been here before, and this time you're not scared. So you just look at it, smile, and shout maniacally "Bring it on motherfucker! Yee fucking haaagh!".

✹ ✷ ✺

Acknowledgements

First of all I'd like to thank my lovely wife, Erin, for having the guts to take me on and the patience to put up with me. That's just in general, nothing to do with kids.

I'd like to thank my mum and dad for giving me such a happy childhood. Although the prospect of attempting to recreate it for my own wee family is a little daunting, at least I know what I should be aiming for.

To all of the people who read the manuscript on its way to completion, I thank you too. Sophie Costello, Jess Holder, Geoffrey Bartlett, Euan Mackay, Ged Gillmore, Irene, Harry and Gillian MacLeod – all off you added a little bit along the way, and encouraged me to finish the bloody thing too.

And finally, although she almost killed me in the process, [Editor's note: Grain of salt, dear readers; grain of salt.] I'd like to thank my editor Shelley Kenigsberg. We all need a little bit of advice now and again, even if it's hard to take, and this is a much better book because of her guidance.

Thank you to all of these people, and thank you, to the one little person I haven't mentioned as yet. Thank you, thank you, thank you.

Resources And Reading Material

Baby on Board, Understanding what your baby needs
  Howard Chiltern, Finch Publishing, 2003
  ISBN-10: 1876451394

Your Pregnancy
  Sydney Ultrasound for Women, 2009

Metabolic Hypothesis for Human Alacrity
  Holly M. Dunsworth, Anna G. Warrener, Terrence Deacon, Peter T. Ellison and Herman Pontzerd.
  E-Published, Proceedings of the National Academy of Science of the United States of America
  (www.pnas.org) 2012

Mothers and Others: The Evolutionary Origins of Mutual Understanding
  Sarah Blaffer Hrdy, Harvard University Press, 2009
  ISBN-10: 0674060326

Baby Love
  Robin Parker, Pan Macmillan Australia, 2009
  ISBN: 9781742613307

Fed Up: Understanding How Food Affects Your Child and What You Can Do About It
  Sue Dengate, Random House Australia, 2008
  ISBN: 9781741667257

Printed in Poland
by Amazon Fulfillment
Poland Sp. z o.o., Wrocław